window style

window style

BLINDS CURTAINS SCREENS SHUTTERS

MARY FOX LINTON

SPECIAL PHOTOGRAPHY BY PIA TRYDE

conran
OCTOPUS

For Lucy, Claire and Anna.
First published in 2000 by Conran Octopus Limited
a part of Octopus Publishing Group
2–4 Heron Quays, London E14 4JP
www.conran-octopus.co.uk

Text copyright © 2000 Jane Bolsover
Original projects copyright© 2000 Mary Fox Linton
Book design and layout copyright
© 2000 Conran Octopus Limited
Special photography copyright
© 2000 Conran Octopus Limited

Commissioning editors Denny Hemming,
Suzannah Gough
Managing editors Lindsay Porter, Catriona Woodburn
Art editors Alison Fenton, Megan Smith,
Isabel de Cordova
Jacket design Carl Hodson
Stylist Cathy Sinker
Picture researchers Claire Taylor, Marissa Keating
Production controllers Sarah Tucker, Alex Wiltshire

British Library Cataloguing-in-Publication Data.
A catalogue record for this book is available from
the British Library.

ISBN: 1 84091-129-8

Printed in China

Author's Acknowledgments
I should like to thank all those who have given their
time and expertise to make this book possible. In
particular, Francesca Harrison, who did more than me
to make this book possible, for without her help there
would be no book. To everyone at Conran Octopus,
both past and present, who remained calm and
pleasant while I was being difficult and too selective.

In addition I should like to thank the following
for allowing us to use their homes for photography,
and in the case of Mrs Yip her designs for the silk
wall project: Mr and Mrs Von Peltz, Mr and Mrs
Bonfiglio, Professor and Mrs Barker, Professor and
Mrs Yip, Mr and Mrs Meekings and Linden Homes.

To the following companies for their generosity
in allowing us to borrow their furniture, rugs and
accessories: Fox Linton Furniture, Wool Classics and
Yeowood South and to Mick Porter of Deanswood
Contract Furnishings for making blinds and curtains
to all shapes and sizes. To Tim Allen for the use of
his painting. And finally to all the other suppliers
who provided fabrics and accessories for the projects
in this book, detailed in the Suppliers list on page 159.

Picture Acknowledgments in page order
10 Henry Wilson/The Interior Archive(Design:
Florence Lim); 11 Andrew Wood/The Interior
Archive(Owner: David Edgell); 12 Alexande Van
Berge; 13 above right Christian Sarramon; 13 below
left Cameron P.R.(Eclectics); 14 Christian
Sarramon(Mercedes Stefani); 14 below left Nicolas
Tosi/Marie Claire Maison (Stylist: Julie Bergeand);
15 above right Luc Wauman; 18 Ray Main/Mainstream;
22 Peter Aprahamian; 23 Alan Weintraub/Arcaid;
24 Polly Wreford; 25 Nicolas Tosi/Marie Claire Maison
(Stylist: Josee Postic); 26 Andrew Wood/The Interior
Archive; 27 Henry Wilson/The Interior Archive
(Stylist: Ann Burri); 32 ipc magazines/Homes
and Gardens(Tom Leighton); 33 Creation Baumann;
36 Guy Obijn; 37 above right Verity Welsted/Robert
Harding(Inspirations); 37 below left Polly
Wreford/ipc magazines/Living etc; 40 left Lucinda
Symons/Robert Harding; 41 left Minh & Wass
(Architects: Tsao & McKown); 41 right Minh & Wass
(Architects: Tsao & McKown); 48 Nicolas Tosi/Marie
Claire Maison(Design: Josee Postic); 49 Christian
Sarramon; 52 Ray Main/Mainstream; 53 Marie-Louise
Avery/Robert Harding; 54 left I.L. Sullivan/Marie
Claire Maison(Stylist: Josee Postic); 54 right Polly
Wreford/ipc magazines; 55 David Parmiter/Robert
Harding; 60 Luc Wauman; 61 above Tim Griffith/
Vogue Living April 98 p.40; 61 below Christian
Sarramon (A.Franchet); 62 left Cameron P.R.(Eclectics);
62 right T.Buckingham/ipc magazines; 63 Annabel
Elston/World of Interiors; 64 left David Parmiter/
Robert Harding; 64 right Paul Ryan/International
Interiors(Design: Jacqueline Morabito); 65 left Morel
M.Pierre/Marie Claire Maison(Stylist: Rosensztroch
Daniel); 65 right Polly Wreford/ipc magazines;
68 Cameron P.R.(Eclectics); 69 Cameron P.R.(Eclectics);
72 Fritz von der Schulenburg/The Interior Archive;
73 Peter Clarke/Vogue Living; 78 Ray Main/
Mainstream; 79 Earl Carter/Belle Magazine;
80 E.Munoz/La Casa de Marie Claire; 81 Michel
Venera/Conrad Original Sunshades; 86 Courtesy of
Mary Fox Linton; 87 left Nicolas Tosi/Marie Claire
Maison(Stylist Josee Postic); 87 right Christian
Sarramon; 90 Trevor Mein/Vogue Living; 91 left
Andrew Wood/The Interior Archive; 91 right Ray
Main/Mainstream; 92 Ray Main/Mainstream; 92-93
Verne Fotografie; 93 right ParkerHobart Ass; 94 Mark
Luscombe-Whyte(Design: Christian de Falbe); 95 MP
Morel/Marie Claire Maison(Stylist: Josee Postic); 100
left Limbour Bertrand/Marie Claire Maison(Stylist:
Ardouin Catherine); 100 right Peter Aprahamian;
101 left Gilles Chabeinex/Marie Claire Maison(Stylist:
Ardouin/Billaud); 101 right Ken Hayden/The Interior
Archive(Design: Jonathan Reed)

CONTENTS

Introduction   6

1 BONE STRUCTURE   8

2 DRESSING UP   20
Curtains   22
Sheers   52
Blinds   60
Combinations   78
Screens & Shutters   90

3 ADDING DETAIL   106

4 MAKING UP   118

Glossary   158
Suppliers   159
Index   160

INTRODUCTION

Although I love fabric, for both colour and texture, I have never felt that curtains are essential to enhance a room. In fact, there are occasions when they definitely detract from a view or from the architectural features of a window. In most homes, however, some form of window covering is essential either for privacy or warmth, and this book introduces you to the choices now available; ranging from curtains, sheers, blinds and screens, to combinations of all four.

Initially, window coverings were used for practical purposes, the most obvious being the retaining of heat. Gradually, with the introduction of linen, prints, and silks from the East and Italy, curtaining became more of a decorative feature.

As we have travelled more widely, ideas for window dressings have been adopted from other countries: blinds from India, screens from Japan, festoon blinds from Venice. Since central heating and double glazing now feature in many homes, heavy curtains are no longer required to keep out the cold, enabling us to experiment with new fabrics and simpler ideas and solutions.

The most important aspects of making curtains are that they should be well made and perfectly finished. Attention to detail will give a window covering quality, something I have tried to bring to the designs in this book. A luxury in today's urban living is light and space, and I hope that by reading this book, you will be inspired to find alternative ideas to traditional curtains and alternative ways to retain both light and privacy.

Mary Fox Linton

THIS PAGE *The combination of a free standing screen and Roman blind offers a versatile solution to dressing a window. The screen is placed across the window, as required, for daytime privacy and the blind is lowered at night.*

LEFT *This tall arched window needs little dressing up, it is beautiful in its own right, but for privacy a simple roller blind has been set half way up, allowing the daylight to stream through the top.*

Whether inherently beautiful or simply practical, a window's shape, size and position adds a definite character to the internal architecture of a room.

bone
structure

STANDARD WINDOWS

ABOVE *As standard windows tend to be fairly small, it is important to keep any treatments simple. To maximize the amount of light entering the room, use fabrics that are light both in colour and weight. Roman blinds are one of the cleanest and neatest ways of treating a standard window. In this bright sunny room, the blinds have been set into the window recess and lowered to act as sun-screens.*

Whether you live in a modern home with double glazing, a Victorian terrace with small sash windows or a country cottage, you will probably have at least one standard or smaller window. Unlike other more dramatic window shapes, it is probably more important for standard windows to have some form of window treatment, particularly with the more modern types, as they do not have a lot of character of their own.

A sense of scale is important when dealing with these modest windows, although if a window is out of proportion it can be adjusted using a wider track or longer length curtains, as long as the contrast is not too excessive. Quite often these windows are positioned with radiators underneath, making blinds the best solution both practically and proportionally. Other practical elements, such as whether the window opens inwards or outwards, also need to be taken into consideration. Some cottages have windows set

into deep alcoves, while other houses have windows set very high; in these cases it may not be necessary to curtain them at all. If you have a beautiful view, and do not need privacy, the window can be turned into a decorative feature by painting the frame in a striking colour. Of all the standard windows, sashes are perhaps the best proportioned, and they easily accept most forms of curtaining, blinds and shutters.

When deciding on window treatments for standard windows, remember that simple styles produce the best results. Choose from Roman blinds, roller blinds or shutters or, if you prefer curtains, opt for smaller diameter poles, rather than tracks and pelmets, with headings that are not too deep. Keep fabrics light in colour and weight to maximize the amount of light that comes into the room. A single curtain caught back to one side can make a prettier alternative to a pair of curtains.

THIS PAGE *For modesty and practical reasons a blind is the obvious choice for a bathroom with tall windows. This wooden Venetian blind adds a feeling of warmth and gives a more natural look to the modern bathroom fittings.*

TALL WINDOWS

Tall windows are highly desirable. They are particularly associated with Georgian architecture, a period which is remembered for its elegant proportions and interior decoration. Many modern homes also have tall windows, running from floor to ceiling or on stairwells.

In Georgian houses, tall windows are usually found on the first floor, where the formal reception rooms were situated, and they offer superb opportunities for window treatments, ranging from classical formal arrangements to simpler, more contemporary styles. One of the great charms of tall windows is that they let in a lot of light. Curtain designs should therefore concentrate on their light-giving properties and not go for over-complicated styles that cover up the beauty of the windows.

RIGHT *The tall windows in this bay have been treated with individual curtains, which allow the light to filter through. The dense fabric borders set against the wall do not obstruct the light.*

BELOW *To complete the modern interior created in this room, the tall Georgian windows have been screened with blue, narrow-slatted Venetian blinds, which offset the elegant frames perfectly.*

If using curtains, don't skimp on fabric; make sure they are generous, and scoop them back with tiebacks or Italian stringing, to allow plenty of light into the room. If you live in an older property which still has the original shutters, use a simple sheer drape, or top the shutters with a single pull-up blind. If using blinds with tall windows, set them within the recess to reveal the frame.

Unfortunately, not all tall windows conform to the Georgian proportions, and in such cases curtaining can be problematic. For rooms with low ceilings, curtains need to be designed so that they bring the eye down and away from the top of the window. Do this by using a deep pelmet, a valance, or curtains with tiebacks set down low.

Not all tall windows are floor-length as some have radiators set against the wall beneath them. However, these windows should still be dressed with full-length curtains for the best decorative effect.

WIDE WINDOWS

ABOVE *With its series of large picture windows down each side, this room has an interesting curtain arrangement. Heavy-duty chrome cable has been stretched along the length of each wall from which lightweight sheers have been suspended at intervals, providing sun screening as it is required.*

The extensive variety of window styles seen in homes today is a direct result of the improvements in glass-making skills over the last few centuries. During the 17th century, windows were composed of small panes of glass patched together in frameworks. When plate glass was developed in the 19th century, windows could be made from several larger panes, or even one large single pane. As technology improved, glazing costs were reduced and windows became much larger; this culminated in the 1950s and 1960s with enormous picture windows, encompassing a whole wall with a single pane of glass, which were designed to bring the view into the room. These wide windows need a different approach to window dressing.

If placed in a good location, picture windows can be a striking feature that needs little embellishment. Unfortunately, this is not always the case, and some form of screening is often required for privacy during the day. Even if the view is beautiful, at night this will turn into a large black hole, so some form of window covering is desirable. Another practical consideration is insulation. Vast areas of single sheet glass are not effective at retaining heat; double glazing can help, but curtaining offers an easy solution.

Simplicity is the key to curtaining picture windows; avoid anything fussy like swags and tails which detract from the view. A single curtain hung simply from a plain pole or pelmet and stacked back to one side avoids the look of a pair of stage curtains. Alternatively, the clean lines of Roman or roller blinds make a good option; practically, however, picture windows often incorporate hinged or sliding doors, so blinds must be able to clear the window fully.

Wide windows made from several panes of glass can be dressed successfully with a series of blinds. These add interest to the window as they can be lowered to varying levels, breaking up the monotony of a continuous horizontal line. Sill-length curtains can be used on windows that are wider than they are high, although floor-length ones tend to work better by balancing the proportions.

Plain fabrics work best on wide windows. Avoid small fussy prints which simply do not work over a large area. Instead, use bolder and more flamboyant designs, whether they be abstract, naturalistic, geometric or stripes. If your view is unpleasant and daytime screening is required, keep it simple. Use a plain voile or muslin that diffuses the light and reduces the outlook to a softened blur; lace fabrics here would be just too much.

ABOVE *Paper thin, sheer fabric Roman blinds add visual interest to this glass wall, and give a versatile solution for screening off sections. When down, the blinds form a fabric wall.*

LEFT *With its unusual angled shape at the centre and monochromatic faces transferred on to each panel, this window provides its own unique treatment.*

ABOVE *French windows and glazed doors that open directly on to a garden or balcony bring the outdoors inside in a unique way and are a delightful asset to a house or apartment.*

RIGHT *Traditionally styled French windows with shutters allow the light to be totally blocked out from the outside, so there is no need for the window to be completely curtained. Gauzy sheers on hinged rods are a perfect choice to filter the daylight and soften the stark blackness when the shutters are closed at night.*

GLASS DOORS

Glazed doors usually open out on to a garden, terrace or balcony, making a beautiful link with the outside world. Further glazed panels, positioned at the sides of or above the doors, are frequently used to make a larger overall window area.

Glazed doors first made their appearance as French windows in 17th-century French mansions, originally opening out on to the upper balconies. In the 19th century they grew in popularity and, at the same time, moved down to the ground floor. Originally, glass doors were simply embellished with stiffened lambrequims – pieces of drapery hung over the top of the window. These followed the shape of the window and often hung down to the floor at the sides, leaving the window itself unencumbered.

It can be difficult deciding what treatment to use for glazed doors. If your view is beautiful and you are not overlooked in any way, ask yourself whether you need to add a window treatment at all. Most of us are not that lucky, and a mixture of both practical and aesthetic considerations influence how you dress glass doors. By definition, glazed doors need to be flexible: the most important criterion is their ability to open and close easily, but you may also want to filter or maximize the amount of daylight coming through the doors, provide some degree of privacy or block out any draughts. The type of window treatment you choose needs to look stylish while performing all the functions you have set for it.

If your glazed doors open outwards, then adding a window treatment is easier, as the doors will not be obstructed. Ones which open inwards need more consideration. Any poles and pelmets must be suspended above the top of the window frame and the curtains need to be pulled far enough back at the

sides so they do not catch in the doors. Alternatively, for a more understated look, lightweight cotton or muslin curtains can be attached to small rods that are fixed to the doors themselves, enabling them to move with the door. Likewise, panels and Roman or roller blinds could be used on glass doors in the same way. If you want to make more of a window feature using this method, add a pair of dress curtains above the glass doors; but you will need to make sure that they hang well clear of the door opening so as not to cause an unnecessary obstruction.

ABOVE Roller blinds provide a versatile option for glazed doors. When lowered, they form a neat unobtrusive screen allowing for privacy at night, and, when raised, they clear the window completely causing no obstructions.

AWKWARD WINDOWS

ABOVE *With their acute angles and corners, rectangular bays can pose something of a challenge. Here, however, separate wooden Venetian blinds have been used for each section of the window. The clean lines produce a contemporary look which also emphasizes the proportions of the bay.*

Many houses possess at least one unusually shaped, or oddly positioned window. When it comes to deciding on a treatment for these windows there are no general rules to follow as each window needs to be looked at individually. These awkward windows add character to a home, so they need to be enhanced and not just covered up with a standard solution.

Bow and bay windows can vary greatly in size from simple alcoves to room-sized projections embracing a whole wall. Today there are tracks available that curve to fit directly into the bay, enabling you to treat the whole window as one unit, although deep bays may need individual blinds or curtains.

Arched and circular windows are often beautiful features in their own right. Luckily, circular windows are often small and do not necessarily need any covering at all. The best approach for arched windows is to use a fixed heading on curtains or blinds, shaped to fit the curve of the arch.

Casement windows are found in old cottages, recessed into thick walls. They tend to be small, and often open inwards. The most practical solution here are curtains set outside the recess, so as not to obstruct the opening or restrict the light.

Dormer windows project from a roof line and have sloping sides. Roman or roller blinds work best for these windows, although special hinged rods can be bought for curtains to swing clear of the glass. Skylights are often set on an angle in the roof. Roller blinds are the best solution for these. Any curtains and blinds used will have to be adapted to fit close to the slope, using poles, cords, rings or clips.

dressing up

There are many different styles of window decorations and coverings to choose from, including curtains, blinds, sheers and screens, and even combinations of all four.

CURTAINS

The generic term 'curtains' covers a wide variety of decorative fabric window treatments, all of which form a screen between you and the outside world. They can be as simple as gathered or pleated lengths of fabric hung straight from a curtain track or pole, or more complicated draped and swagged styles, complete with pelmets and tiebacks. Aesthetically, curtains not only soften or emphasize the architectural qualities of a window and provide a focal point in the room, but also add colour, texture, pattern, and a sense of warmth and intimacy to a room. Practically, they keep out the light, insulate the room against cold and significantly reduce noise.

Curtains are a fairly recent addition to windows. It was not until the second half of the seventeenth century, with the development of the sash window, that the French first began to exploit the decorative potential of curtains. Before this most windows were small, making light a premium; they were also usually inward-opening, so curtains were not the most practical option. If used, curtains were simply lengths of cotton or linen that could be pulled across the window, purely to filter light.

With the development of larger windows, curtains assumed a new flamboyant character. Pairs of curtains, instead of single drapes, began to be used for the first time, and pelmets were developed to hide the rods and rings. The early Georgian period saw the emergence of the single curtain that pulled up into a soft, billowy drape beneath a pelmet. From the late eighteenth through to the early nineteenth centuries, asymmetrical draping became popular, followed by divided curtains once again, while poles, rings, finials and tiebacks became more decorative and conspicuous. During the nineteenth century, curtains became excessively elaborate with lots of layers. These lavish draperies incorporated vast amounts of fabric, braids, fringes, ropes and tassels. The Victorians

ABOVE *These elegant unlined curtains, with a deep hand-smocked heading, hang beneath a mock cornice which hides the track and mechanism and follows the curve of the windows.*

LEFT *Sun-rooms form a link with the outside world, and covering the windows can detract from their purpose. Here, simple screening is achieved by using lightweight unlined curtains which draw across the windows, as required, to form a wall of fabric.*

While old ideas re-emerged and were continually re-interpreted, it was the elegant old designs that remained rather than those characterized by excess.

The choice of fabrics and styles of curtaining available today is almost infinite. They can be made to suit any type of window, they can be of any length, lined or unlined, lightly gathered or full, and can hang freely or be draped more formally. The way curtains hang depends partly on the type of heading you choose, which can range from a simple gathered top, sleek pencil pleats and more formal hand-made French pleats to, at the other extreme, plain looped tab tops.

It is the architecture of a room, particularly the style and proportions of the windows and their surrounds, that give a framework in which to work when you come to choose a style of curtain. As a general rule, curtains should always be floor length unless the window is particularly small, in which case perhaps a blind or other window treatment would be preferable. If you have a radiator beneath a window and are unable to move it, floor-length curtains are still the best option. Keep them pulled well back during the day, and, as long as they are not interlined, the heat should still pass through the fabric at night.

Most styles of curtain can be made successfully in any fabric; it is the choice of style and fixtures which will do more to determine the overall effect. The simple approach to curtaining is often the best; less can definitely be more. Simplicity need not be austere or unwelcoming; it is having the confidence to let the fabric speak for itself rather than cluttering it up with decorative details that is important. A restrained approach to fabrics can work equally well in both grand and more humble interiors. When choosing your fabric, consider both colour and pattern, always keeping in mind the mood you want to create.

ABOVE *Simple, unlined curtains form informal pools on the floor, in keeping with the fresh and youthful style of the room.*

RIGHT *Effective but basic, these long, flat muslin panels are threaded on to hinged rods that swing clear of the inward-opening windows.*

took this to extremes with heavy, dark curtains, usually trailing to the floor and blocking out as much light as possible. This style was taken as a sign of status; if a man's family could live without bright daylight, it meant that they did not have to work for a living.

As is usually the case there was a reaction to this excess, and in the twentieth century curtains began to play a much more pared-down role, becoming generally simpler and lighter. During the last century a unique diversity of styles emerged, but the trend towards less weighty arrangements has remained.

THIS PAGE *Windows are designed to let light in and, depending on the type of fabric chosen, light is filtered to varying degrees, offering the opportunity to enhance the quality of light, evoke an atmosphere, create patterns, or even alter colours. This interestingly woven raffia-type fabric is one of an ever-growing range of decorative sheer alternatives available today.*

LEFT *Fabric choice plays an important role in the way window treatments influence a room. Textural interest can be used to reinforce the impressions already prevalent in a room. Velvets, as shown here, evoke a sense of luxury; with their weight and thickness they make gorgeously rich curtains. Other textures promote different moods: soft woollens offer a comforting feel, cottons and linen give a crisp, cool look.*

FABRICS

Fabric choice is a matter of personal taste, but there are so many fabrics on the market today that it is difficult to know where to start looking. There are heavy linens, textured weaves, silks, thick velvets and fine lawns, to name but a few. Once you have decided on the type of fabric, you need to think about colour and pattern. Colour might be determined by the decor of your room, but will you want traditional florals, glazed chintzes, small geometrics or stripes?

Many people are drawn to a piece of fabric purely by its appearance, but you also need to think of its texture, how it handles, drapes or folds, and whether it creases easily. You need to be aware of how the fabric is affected by light, whether it is opaque, dense, reflective or transparent. Try imagining the fabric in its proposed setting and decide whether it is suitable in practical terms for the style that you intend to make.

The real starting point to choosing a fabric is to make sure that it feels right for the job. Take several samples home and when you have decided on your favourite, either borrow a large sample from the shop, or invest in a metre length. The colour will look denser in a larger piece and patterns can look totally different when viewed from a distance. Hang up your piece of fabric, drape it, fold it, and see how it reacts. View it in both natural and artificial light, and think about the size of the pattern repeats. Finally, remember not to skimp on the fabric quantity; generous full curtains in a cheaper fabric look so much better than curtains made with half the amount of a more expensive fabric.

You can be very imaginative with curtain fabrics. Experiment with upholstery and clothing fabrics, leather, throws, rugs, antique fabrics, and even paper or wire mesh for screens or blinds.

Country Flannel Curtain

Furnishings made from clothing fabrics are currently very fashionable, whether as sweater-like cushions or sofas upholstered in men's suiting. Here a tweedy jacket fabric, trimmed with contrasting tan leather, creates a curtain that is 'smart country', but you could equally choose a pinstripe suiting with black leather trim for a chic city look (see page 131 for making up instructions). This fabric works well unlined, whether as a single curtain or a pair for French windows or doors. Since short curtains in these blanket-type fabrics tend to look rather mean, it is advisable to make them long enough to brush the floor.

You can accentuate the country look by using tan leather and suede trimmings. The leading edge of the curtain is bound with mock suede, and the curtain is

RIGHT & FAR RIGHT *Men's tweed, herringbone or pinstripe suiting offer a wonderful selection of warm fabrics from which to create this fabulous curtain.*

BELOW *A strip of fabric edged with suede forms a complementary tieback. It is simply wrapped around the curtain and secured in place with a touch-and-close fastener. Leather buttons complete the look.*

hung using strong leather tabs. Although these tabs are ready-made, with a silver stud on the front and a wire hook that pushes through the fabric to secure the curtain to the pole, you could make your own tabs from leather or mock suede.

When drawn back, the curtain can either be left to hang loosely at the side of the window or held in place with a tieback. To continue the clothing theme, make the tieback from the curtain fabric, bind the edges in mock suede and decorate it with two leather buttons.

To finish off the look, hang the curtain from a polished metal curtain pole with tan leather finials – something reminiscent of a shooting stick.

POSSIBLE FABRIC COMBINATIONS
Tweed and mock suede
Pinstripe and fake leather
Tartan and leather
Flannel and velvet
Tartan and felt

RIGHT *Clear access is an important consideration for French windows. This curtain hangs from a brass pole that runs the entire width of the room, allowing the curtain to be pulled back and rest against the wall at the side.*

BELOW *Other fabrics in the room pick up the rich colours of this luxurious printed silk, pulling together the overall scheme.*

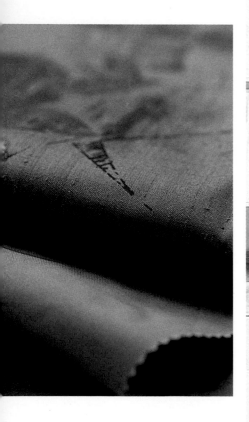

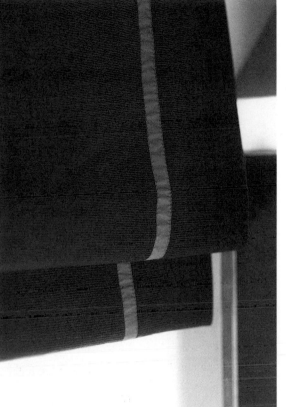

FAR LEFT *At night, the room is completely transformed into a dramatic stage set as the drawn curtain forms a fabulous wall of silk, perfect for dining in style.*

LEFT *You can combine different fabrics in the same room by coordinating colours. This Roman blind is made from cotton, trimmed with silk ribbons, making it a more practical fabric for the kitchen end of the room.*

Wall of Silk

Rich colours and fabrics echo the Orient and create a sumptuous, exotic atmosphere. This room is a basement kitchen/dining room, so it is preferable not to block out any daylight from the French windows. During the day the curtain pulls back to one side, away from the glass, to rest against the wall, but at night, with a wonderful wall of fabric covering the windows, the room is transformed into a dramatic stage setting, making it a perfect environment for entertaining (see page 132 for making up instructions).

This large fully-lined curtain, made from a luxurious printed silk, has a handmade pencil-pleat heading. The curtain is hung from a brass pole, which is fitted close to the ceiling and matches the door

fixtures, and which spans the whole width of the room. If you want to use a delicate fabric like silk, hang the curtain from a ready-corded pole or use a separate curtain pull to draw it across, otherwise the the leading edge of the fabric is likely to get soiled quite quickly as it is drawn to and fro.

Although the silk fabric is ideal for the French windows at the dining end and creates a very opulent feel, it is impractical for the kitchen window at the opposite end of the room. A Roman blind can be made of cotton to complement the curtains by picking out a couple of the colours from the silk . The seats of the dining room chairs could be covered in the same harder-wearing fabric to complete the theme.

POSSIBLE FABRIC COMBINATIONS

Silk and cotton

Taffeta and textured slub silk

Damask and cotton or linen union

Silk or polyester

EDGING & TRIMS

Fringes, braids, borders, tassels, binding and other kinds of embellishments are all ideas for adding interest to window treatments. Purely decorative, edgings and trims can provide contrasting colour and texture to curtains, blinds, pelmets and tiebacks. Edgings help to define the shape of a curtain or blind, and they can either be added to all sides of a project, or just to one edge. When adding decorative details, choose them carefully and apply them neatly. The details should be used to emphasize the overall line of the window treatment, and should not be too fancy or fussy. Over-decoration will spoil the effect.

Borders are usually made from a fabric, ribbon, bias binding or braid that contrasts with the main fabric. A border should be sympathetic to the fabric to which it is being applied, in terms of weight, stitchability, and washability. Borders can be flat, frilled, pleated or piped, and several sorts can be used at once. Care needs to be taken when judging the proportions of a border; always try to match the scale of the finishing touches to the scale of the whole project.

Fringes come in many forms, from those suitable for really grand, elegant window treatments, to less formal styles. Block fringes are fine and dense with a silky appearance; they are often multi-coloured and can be quite deep. Bullion fringes, on the other hand, are heavier. Made from thick, twisted cords with a rich opulent feel, these are more suitable for long, heavy drapes. There is also available today a wide variety of bejewelled, knotted, tasselled and quirky pompom fringes in various widths and large colour ranges.

Another way to decorate your window treatments is to add individual details. Tassels and cords look stylish with more formal drapery, but look out for unusual, less traditional ways to emphasize edges or

create designs, such as beads, appliqué, crystals from an old chandelier or pieces of mirror that catch the light. Other more fussy embellishments include fabric bows, rosettes or Maltese crosses, which can add three-dimensional qualities. Use these trimmings more sparingly though, as they can look dated. Whatever you choose, stick to one theme throughout.

ABOVE *An interesting, almost wind-chime effect has been created on the hem of this sheer curtain, by attaching assorted pieces of coloured velvet which glint and shine as they catch the sunlight.*

Suiting & Satin

By using the same fabric combinations in different locations for curtains and blinds, you can successfully link two areas. This can be seen in this apartment with its galleried bedroom, where the upper and lower windows are visible from the ground floor.

The contrast created between the matt and shine of the two fabrics used becomes the main decorative theme for these curtains and blinds. This smart tailored look is achieved using a soft, warm wool and mohair suiting for the main fabric, and a cool shiny satin to define the edges of both the curtains and blinds (see page 134 for making up instructions).

ABOVE LEFT & RIGHT
The same contrast border is used to define the edges of both the curtains and blinds.

LEFT *The wide bedroom window is spanned by three separate but matching Roman blinds which work together in unison.*

RIGHT *As the upper and lower windows in this apartment are both visible from the ground floor, it was important that the window treatments unified the two areas. The ideal solution was to use the same fabrics, but in ways that worked practically for the two different areas.*

The French windows on the ground floor are dressed with simple unlined curtains with a slight gathered heading and bound leading edges and hems. The heading itself is hidden behind the plaster coving that runs around the outer edges of the ceiling. The window in the bedroom area is wide with a radiator below it, so Roman blinds were the best option. To cover the full width of the window, three separate blinds were needed, but to make them easy to operate they were corded so that they can be raised or lowered as one. The blinds are fully lined, but as this is the sleeping area additional darkness could be guaranteed by using blackout lining. The clean-lined edging on the blinds, neatly mitred at the corners with no visible stitching showing on the right side of the blinds completes the smart, tailored look.

POSSIBLE FABRIC COMBINATIONS
Wool worsted and satin
Basic weave cottons and cotton sateen
Machine-woven tapestry and silk

HEADINGS

A heading runs horizontally across the top of the window treatment and attaches the curtain or blind to some form of support; it also determines how the fabric hangs. Curtains generally have more fabric in them than the width of the window, so they need to be gathered at the top. Today, there are lots of interesting ways to hang curtains besides the more traditional methods and curtain tape is often used, although some types of heading are still best stitched by hand. With blinds, the choice is not so wide; being flat, blinds are usually fastened to a timber

RIGHT & BELOW It is easy to turn an ordinary curtain into something special. These two decorative headings are simple and effective. The metal clips threaded on to a pole allow the curtain to be pegged up like washing, while eyelets in the top of a curtain allow it to be threaded on a tension wire.

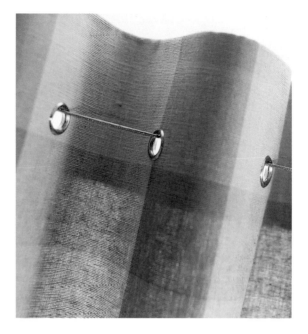

support with touch-and-close tape for easy removal, or decorative studs for a more permanent solution.

Always make sure that your chosen heading is suitable for the fabric. The most basic headings can be simple but decorative, making a feature of the suspension. These headings use the least amount of fabric, and the curtain hangs like a panel. Choose from a slot heading sewn along the top of a curtain, or a row of tabs, hooks or ties threaded on to a pole. Decorative peg-like metal clips or eyelet headings are ideal for curtains that are not often pulled back.

Ready-made heading tapes with draw-cords give both informal and elegant results. Standard gathered tape gives a shallow, random gather – a heading suitable for informal, unlined curtains. A pencil-pleat heading is probably the most popular choice; it gives stiff, regular, close-packed pleats. There are also tapes available for making formal French, box and goblet pleats, but these look far better if they are stitched by hand. The more decorative headings can be left on view, while plainer ones are best concealed by a pelmet or drapery.

Pole & Eyelet Heading

Large metal eyelets, piercing a curtain heading and threaded along a chrome curtain pole, give a fresh contemporary look to a room and provide a method of hanging curtains both practical and attractive.

Daylight diffuses beautifully through the centre panel of the closed curtain, casting a warm glow while still providing for privacy. Drawn back from the window, the curtain takes up little wall space, thus letting in the maximum amount of sunlight. It is a perfect style for a dressing room or bathroom, as you can repeat the eyelet effect on a shower curtain or on curtains hung to cover cupboards. Equally you can scale down the idea in size for smaller cottage-style windows, by using a narrower pole and smaller eyelets.

This curtain, made from heavy-weight unlined calico fabric, has checked borders along the leading edge, top and base. The deeper border along the base gives weight to the curtain, both physically and visibly, and balances the chunkiness of the pole (see page 136 for instructions on how to make them).

To make sure the curtain hangs well, choose fabrics of similar weights for both the main panel and the border. To make the curtain without a contrasting border, choose a heavier weight of fabric, perhaps one with an interesting texture, but keep it plain-coloured and clean-looking by avoiding florals or fabrics with busy patterns.

LEFT *The substantial borders on this curtain give crisp definition to its shape, and the plain and checked fabrics make an eyecatching contrast. In addition to adding weight to the curtain, the double thickness border frames the lightweight central panel, enhancing the light that softly diffuses through.*

POSSIBLE FABRIC COMBINATIONS

Heavy-weight calico and woven check

Voile and silk

Muslin and calico

Chambray and denim

LEFT *Eyelets threaded on to a chunky chrome pole create a modern contemporary look, which is perfect for curtains that are not pulled back often. You can buy eyelets from most department stores or specialist shops in a variety of sizes, along with a tool for their insertion. Very large eyelets, however, need to be inserted by specialist companies.*

TIEBACKS

The tiebacks of a window treatment have both practical and decorative features. Practically, they scoop the curtain fabric back gracefully to let more light into the room, correcting the proportions of the curtains, creating a degree of fullness and giving them additional shape. In decorative terms, tiebacks can be used to alter a whole look or pull it together. It is best to team busy curtains with minimal tiebacks, whereas simple curtains can easily carry off fabulous oversized tiebacks.

There are both hard and soft tiebacks available. Historically, hard tiebacks – sometimes called holdbacks or brackets – were very popular and it is possible to find some lovely antique examples at a price. There are also plenty of contemporary designs from which to choose. Made from cast metals or wood, they are either curved in a U-shape like a large hook, or have a straight shaft that extends out from the wall with a decorative boss on the front, over which the curtain is draped. You could also use your imagination and look out for fun alternatives, such as glass door knobs and door knockers, but make sure they are practical.

Soft tiebacks can be made either from fabric or cord, and are usually looped around a concealed hook on the wall. At one time, shaped and stiffened fabric tiebacks were popular, but these are now somewhat dated. The simplest fabric tieback is a long narrow strip of fabric that can be tied in a bow around the curtain, or looped over the hook. Ready-made rope and cord tiebacks are one of the neatest forms. Plain or tasselled, they add a luxurious feel to the curtain. In fact, anything that is long enough can be used as a tieback; experiment with chains of beads, strings of shells, or skeins of raffia, depending on your room.

FAR LEFT & LEFT This fabulous rope-and-tassel tieback, decorated with contrasting feathers, makes a beautiful foil to the simple plain curtain beneath. It is important to ensure that this sort of tieback is thick and heavy enough for the weight of your curtains. The stunning glass holdback is actually made from the top section of a telegraph pole; look out for other unusual objects to hold your curtains away from the window.

ABOVE & LEFT *These formal unlined curtains are bordered with gold ribbon along the leading edge, and held back from the window with long, fine brackets made from beaten gold metal. These elegant brackets give the appearance of a serpent-like piece of jewellery coiling around the curtain edge.*

RIGHT *The focal point of this simple yet elegant window treatment is its long tasselled tieback and its sparkling glass fob.*

BELOW *This handmade French-pleat heading is both formal and stylish.*

FAR RIGHT *The combination of the beautiful silk dress curtain with a sheer Roman blind allows for privacy during both day and night.*

Aqua & Jewel Tieback

This formal full-length dress curtain, with a deep handmade French-pleat heading, looks extremely elegant on long, tall windows. Set outside the window recess and attached to a shaped pelmet board with touch-and-close tape, the whole curtain gracefully sweeps out in a curve at the centre (see page 137 for making up instructions).

The beautiful aqua-coloured silk is backed with a heavy blackout lining to add weight, thickness and body to the curtain while avoiding the necessity for interlining. The blackout lining is ideal for bedrooms, especially in a city or town where there is street lighting, as it effectively shuts out all light. This curtain would work equally well in a dining room, however, when made in a rich heavy-weight silk or velvet.

During the daytime, the curtain is gently pulled back to one side with a fabulous long, silk-tasselled tieback. Decorated with a beautiful crystal fob, which sparkles like a jewel and picks up the colour of the curtain, the tieback is one of the main features of the window. The curtain, with its clean elegant lines, is a wonderful foil for such an exuberant tieback. A sheer, unlined Roman blind is set into the recess of the window; it allows light in but brings privacy to the bedroom when dressing. The blind is formal in style, and complements the curtain. It has rods in the back so that it folds up neatly when raised and lowered.

POSSIBLE FABRIC COMBINATIONS

Silk taffeta on voile

Velvet on sheer

Cotton chintz on muslin

Damask on lace

Damask on sheer

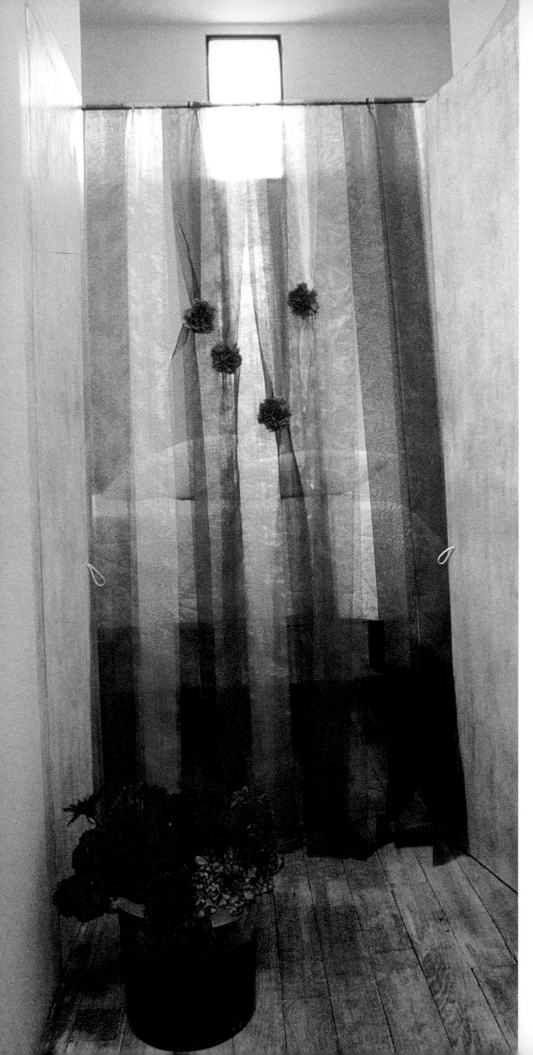

BANNERS

A banner is a flat piece of fabric, much like a flag. It is therefore the perfect vehicle for displaying decorative work. Throughout history, tapestry and patchwork banners, or wall hangings, have been used to decorate and insulate houses and castles. Turning a banner into a window covering is a very simple idea, but one which increases the scope for individual treatments that can transform the most basic window into something special.

Banners can be attached to the window frame on a fixed rail, or swing out on a hinged metal or wooden arm. Alternatively, they can be hooked up and taken down as required. Window banners can also be echoed in other areas of the room: as a covering for an internal door, or as a traditional wallhanging.

Sunlight will be filtered variously, depending on the type of fabric used to make the banner. This provides an opportunity to enhance the quality of the light, create patterns, or evoke an atmosphere. Panels of lace, printed voile or fine muslin let light in but cast a moody, shadowy effect. When there is no need to cover the window fully, experiment with unusual-shaped banners and see how the light is blocked and angled through the day. Banners in coloured fabric act like stained glass, tinting and altering the colours in the rest of the room. Try overlapping coloured fabrics to achieve an effect like a wall painting.

Hanging lots of narrow banners together gives the appearance of flags and a slightly military feel. Try adding ribbons, or use old Indian fabrics, embroidered panels or shawls to evoke a sense of luxury. In total contrast, for a clean, ultra-modern look, you could choose materials such as mesh and plastic. Whatever you select, the main criterion for a banner is that the fabric pieces remain flat.

ABOVE *With their geometric panels of colour, these banners create a crisp, stylish effect. Simply cut from plastic film, the banners are fixed in place with spray adhesive to provide interesting screening with a striking mix of colours.*

RIGHT *Gauzy fabric banners in hot reds and bright oranges bring a liveliness to this room. When the window is open, the slightest air movement is enough to make the banners waft gently to and fro. Coloured banners filter out strong sunlight, and warm the room on cold, bleak days. To ring the changes, simply loop the banners over tiebacks at each side.*

LEFT *These pink, purple and orange banners combine stunning decorative value with effective, simple screening. To allow a little extra sunlight through, some of the fabric is gathered at varying heights and clipped with paper flowers.*

ABOVE *You could make a range of interchangeable banners using colours from a piece of art so that you could swap them to suit your mood.*

RIGHT *This sophisticated window treatment looks especially good in a city context. The fullness of the curtains gives a softness to the window which, with the monochromatic colour scheme, might otherwise appear stark. Use this style on full-length or French windows, where the curtains can graze the floor and the banners can be shown to their best effect.*

Bright Stripes

Simplicity is the key to this style. A pair of full-length white poplin curtains has been given a dramatic accent – in the form of boldly coloured detachable banners. To achieve the maximum effect, the curtains must be hung on tall or French windows so that they brush the floor and allow the banners to billow out in the slightest breeze. The whole look is clean, fresh and easy to achieve.

The flat banners are made from strips of stiff linen fabric, attached to the top edge of the gathered curtain with touch-and-close tape. The two curtains are then hung from a single track, which allows them to be drawn across the window without disturbing the banners. A narrow fabric-covered or painted wooden pelmet discreetly hides the track and fixings (see page 139 for instructions on how to make up).

Originally designed to flatter rather than compete with the large painting, the choice of banner colours reflect the colours used by the artist.

RIGHT Changing the colour of the banner transforms completely the feel of the room. The red banner works well in the evening, giving a warm, cosy glow under the artificial lighting.

BELOW A fresh spring look is achieved using a yellow banner. This style is so versatile that you can choose to ring the changes following the seasons, and bringing the colours of your garden into your room.

However, one of the fun and versatile aspects of this style is that you can ring the changes by using banners in various colours according to the season or occasion. You might want to bring colours into the room from your garden in springtime or change the banners over the Christmas holidays to add a more festive feel to the room. Keep the look bold and simple by using plain-coloured fabrics, perhaps in interesting textures, to create the most striking effect.

POSSIBLE FABRIC COMBINATIONS

Cotton poplin with linen

Calico with hessian

Toile de Jouy with plain cotton chintz

Silk with brocade

DRESS CURTAINS

ABOVE *A truly no-sew option, this ultra-simple curtain, made from a length of loosely woven cotton scrim with frayed edges, is draped over a pole to create a valance effect, and then gently caught back to one side in a loose swag .*

Dress curtains are fixed curtains that are arranged or dressed to hang at a window or door. Their purpose is to add decorative interest and give definition to a window that does not need curtains for practical reasons. For example, adding a dress curtain to a window which already has shutters for privacy, softens the edges around the window.

Dress curtains can be either formal or informal arrangements and can range from traditionally constructed swag drapes that are lined and interlined, to more simple loose drapes with a more modern feel. Loosely draped effects can be achieved quite easily without any sewing skills at all. You can simply throw a tapestry, blanket, throw or length of voile over a curtain pole, and either let it hang free, or catch it back to one side of the window with a tieback. Alternatively, a long length of fabric can be wrapped round and round the curtain pole to hang down at one or both sides of the window.

If traditional long curtains are not to be drawn at night, they too can be artfully arranged into pools on the floor. Alternatively, pairs of curtains can be permanently joined at the top and caught back high up with Italian stringing or metal tiebacks. This is the perfect solution for arched windows where the top of the curtain needs to echo the shape of the window frame. If privacy is needed at night, drapes can then be combined with working curtains, blinds or shutters.

Dress curtains work well in bay windows; they can be mounted outside the bay to resemble daytime curtains and used in conjunction with blinds to cover the windows. Likewise, on tall windows and landings, a carefully arranged dress curtain can look far better than basic curtains which you have to remember to re-adjust as day turns to night.

LEFT *Nothing could be simpler than these long white muslin panels draped loosely over a wooden pole. They are a perfect foil for this pretty, but rustic bedroom. When the window is open, the gentle breeze makes the curtains billow in and out in a very romantic manner. The curtains can be adjusted to different levels of double thickness, either pooling on the floor or hanging level, altering the tone of light emitted, and the mood of the room.*

THIS PAGE *This dress curtain is formed by hanging an unlined curtain from a wooden pole, and arranging a matching bound-edged throw in deep folds over the top to create an impressive draped heading.*

RIGHT *Use throws and cushions on your furniture that match your curtains to unify the look. You will create a warm, cosy environment by combining natural fabrics, such as knitted cables, loosely woven linens and soft suede.*

FAR RIGHT *These finials are made by covering lengths of chrome tube with fabric and decorative leather strips then slipping them over the pole ends.*

Alpaca Throw

Introducing the cosy, comforting feeling of a throw to a window and creating ties between the curtain and other room furnishings were the inspirations behind this design (see page 140 for making up instructions). The colours used are all creamy and light, except for small touches of coffee. But textures are more important than colours in this interior; warm, soft tactile fabrics are the perfect antidote to a cold room.

The heading is created by draping a throw over a curtain pole, allowing the fabric to hang in soft folds. Because the folds can be disarranged when the curtain is drawn, the throw works best as a dress curtain, used in conjunction with a sheer.

If you have a throw large enough, make the entire curtain from the throw. Alternatively, stitch a separate curtain, lined or unlined, and make a throw to match, plus an extra one to drape on a sofa. The idea is to create the impression that the curtain and heading are made from one piece of fabric. Here the edges of the throw have been bound in a toning mock suede fabric, enhancing the tactile feeling.

To complete the look, customize the ends of the wooden curtain pole. Here chrome tubes that slide over the pole have been covered with a natural linen, pleated to reflect the folds in the throw, and decorated with fine leather strips to tie in with the pole.

POSSIBLE FABRIC COMBINATIONS
Basic plain cotton weaves and suede
Wool worsted and satin
Linen and felt

SHEERS

Sheers are like frosted glass in that they have translucent or semi-translucent qualities, which filter natural light without completely blocking out the view. Besides being practical in providing privacy, screening unappealing views and cutting out the sun's glare, sheers provide tremendous scope for imaginative window treatments, whether gathered into soft feminine curtains, draped as a pelmet, or used as a flat blind.

Muslin and gauze fabrics have been used as sun-screens for hundreds of years, especially in hotter climates. In the seventeenth century, muslin was draped lavishly around windows when most other window treatments were still utilitarian. The Georgians used muslin for their ruched festoon blinds, while in the late eighteenth and early nineteenth century, asymmetrical drapery was combined with the rich heavy-weight curtaining that became popular, and became characteristic of Regency style. During the Industrial Revolution, with the mass production of loom-made lace, there was a switch in popularity from muslin to lace. The Victorians had a passion for truly elaborate draperies, combining heavy curtains with pelmets, swags and tails; they used the delicate lace for under-curtains in these complex arrangements.

Thankfully, the days are now past when everyone felt they had to put up net curtains at their windows to keep out the neighbourhood. After a backlash when people resisted putting anything up at all, there has been a return to using lightweight, see-through curtains for decorative use. Today the choice of textures, fibres and patterns is huge. Not only is there muslin and cotton, but also silks, voiles, gauzes, seersuckers, and a whole range of synthetic translucents – pierced, stitched, beaded. Today the most delicate and decorative of all the sheers can be

LEFT & ABOVE *The translucent quality of sheers and the way they diffuse daylight make them very appealing. With the large choice of see-through fabrics available today, there is an infinite number of possibilities for any room in the house. The fineness of voile means it can be draped in vast quantities to pool on to the floor, or more formally cut and stitched to form delicate sheer panels, decorated with a button trim.*

found in the synthetics, displaying filigree designs and interesting textures. This effect can also be achieved to some degree by using printed muslins, spotted voiles, embroidered organzas or intricate weaves. When scooped up and gathered, striped sheers can create interesting effects as the light plays on the lines. Plain muslin and voile share the same ability to filter light, but with softer, more muted results.

Sheers offer any decorator a wealth of opportunities. They can be draped lavishly over a window, creating a soft romantic mood, or stretched taut over a frame to lend an air of modern, austere elegance. As sheers are so fine, they are very flexible, but because they are so lightweight, sheer curtains only need simple headings.

See-through curtaining does not have to be white. Muslins and laces also come in shades of cream and buttermilk, and other sheers are available in a variety of both soft and deep colours. Remember, though, that some of the inexpensive fabrics in darker shades will fade in the sunlight, so hang them at a window away from direct sun. You can create fabulous stained-glass effects too by overlapping different jewel-coloured sheers which produce other shades as the light shines through.

Easy-care factors are important for sheers, especially in cities where they are often the first defence against dirt and grime. Fabrics made from natural fibres are more delicate than man-made ones, which will withstand frequent washing and do not always need ironing. Many sheers come in wide widths, so that there is no need to join them with ugly seams which show as the light shines through. If your sheer fabrics are not wide enough, combine them with other lightweight fabrics, or create decorative borders that become a feature of the whole curtain.

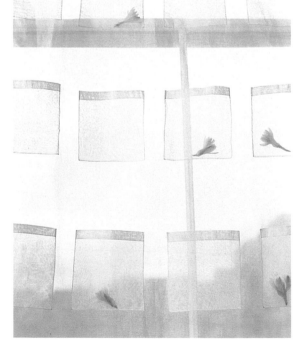

FAR LEFT *Many novelty sheers are now readily available, but this beautiful two-tone fabric could – with a little time and patience – be produced quite simply and cheaply at home.*

LEFT *This sheer fabric curtain has been transformed into a work of art. Dainty square pockets have been stitched in rows on the fabric, while pressed flowers have been dropped into some of the pockets.*

THIS PAGE *This pretty sash window has been delicately covered using an ultra-sheer organza panel to screen the sun. The fresh blue and white colour scheme is cleverly echoed with vertical blue strips of ribbon appliquéd down the curtain.*

THIS PAGE *Sheers are easy to manipulate and can be made without difficulty to fit the shape of an arched window. This white muslin curtain is scooped back with a narrow tieback, so that the light entering the room is partly diffused.*

LEFT *This gently gathered sheer curtain has small tucks stitched along its top edge which is curved to fit the shape of the window frame. It is fixed in place with touch-and-close fastener, making it easy to remove for laundering.*

Long White Sheer

Arched windows are a constant reminder of the architecture of your house, besides being beautiful in their own right. They are difficult to cover with curtains, however. This unlined sheer curtain provides the perfect solution where a degree of privacy is required. Plenty of fabric makes the window appear soft and less austere, but the light still filters through (see page 142 for making up instructions).

The fabric fullness is created by stitching small knife pleats along the top edge. The top of the curtain is cut in an arch to follow the shape of the window, and is fastened in place with touch-and-close tape. One side of the tape is stuck or stapled to the window frame while the other side is stitched to the top edge of the curtain. The tape allows the curtain to be removed easily for cleaning. Although shown on an arched window, this curtain can be adapted to fit a standard straight-edged window.

The curtain can be left to drape loosely over the whole window, or drawn back to one side to allow more light into the room. A thin fabric tieback or a metal hooked tieback can be used to secure the curtain. Alternatively, use the technique known as Italian stringing. Stitch a line of clear plastic rings horizontally across the back of the sheer curtain, at the height you wish the curtain to pull back, and then thread a fine cord through the rings, securing it to the last one. To gather up the curtain, gently pull the cord along the rings and fasten it to a cleat at one side of the window. Unfasten it to let the curtain drape back.

POSSIBLE FABRICS

Cotton voile

Plain muslin

Machine-woven net

Printed or patterned sheers

Silver Beaded Sheers

With its sparkling glass beads and crushed silver fabric, this design is young, fun – almost space age. Yet it also has a quality feel about it. It is definitely a contemporary style that works perfectly with modern chrome furniture. Colour has been kept to a minimum, with just the sharp injection of bright blue glass finials on the pole to complement the upholstery (see page 143 for making up instructions).

Two unlined curtains are hung at the window, one in front of the other. The back curtain is made from a sheer flat panel, decorated with a circle of glass beads. Although this fabric was bought as a ready-beaded panel, it is worth looking at evening and wedding dress fabrics for inspiration: you will get some fabulous ideas. Alternatively, you can stitch beads and sequins on to a plain sheer fabric yourself to create your own one-of-a-kind curtain design.

The front curtain is made from a crushed metallic fabric. It needs to be fairly lightweight so that the light can shine through and illuminate the beadwork. This front piece is fuller than the back panel, and has tucks stitched along the top edge. It is attached to the pole in front with chrome clips that work rather like pegs and then falls to sweep the floor.

LEFT *This curtain style plays with light. The sheer panel with its circle of sparkling beads softly diffuses the light entering the room, while the more opaque crushed silver curtain appears sheer when the light shines through, illuminating the beads behind.*

RIGHT & FAR RIGHT *To enhance the space-age look, the silver curtain is hung from a chunky chrome pole with peg-like clips, while sapphire-blue finials define the ends of the pole. The beautiful sheer panel is embroidered with a circle of small sparkling beads which glint and twinkle in the sunlight.*

This pair of sheers offers several variations of arrangement. The front curtain can hang loose at the side of the window, either fully or partially drawn back, so that all or part of the beaded circle is seen. Alternatively, a simple silver cord can be used to hook both curtains, or just the top one, to one side.

POSSIBLE FABRIC COMBINATIONS

Metallic fabrics with embroidered sheers

Sequined sheers with silk taffeta

Novelty sheers with coloured muslin

BLINDS

Blinds are an extremely popular and versatile form of window treatment. They do not spoil the view and can be used as filters to screen out the daylight to varying degrees, or block out the light totally. Aesthetically, blinds are a clean-edged form of window treatment; their neatness and simplicity does not conflict with the window's style, allowing fancy architraves to remain on show, and other architectural details of the room to take precedence over the window's dressing. Blinds also have many practical advantages. They are an economical alternative to curtains, as they are usually made from a single piece of fabric that covers only the window itself. They are often the best choice for kitchens and bathrooms where full-length curtains are not practical, and are also useful in alcoves, and for awkwardly-shaped and inaccessible windows. They can be made to fit any size of window, and are

ABOVE *This distinctive striped Roman blind has been cleverly constructed by stitching a coarsely woven fabric to strips of sheer.*

FAR LEFT & LEFT *Roman blinds are useful for spanning large areas of glass without using masses of fabric, and they can be corded to work together or individually to create sun-screens for different areas. One solution for an inward-opening window is to fix a cane rolling blind to the outside of the window to act as a sun shield on a hot day.*

particularly good for small ones as they do not block out too much light when raised.

Blinds can be used in other practical ways around the home too: as an alternative to cupboard doors in a kitchen or bedroom, for example, or as informal room dividers.

Most blinds are raised and lowered either by means of a spring mechanism or by a cording system. They can be set flat against the window, or face-fixed outside the recess, either rolling up or rising in a series of horizontal folds, or they can be hooked, ruched, or gathered up in soft, billowing scallops. Used on their own or in conjunction with curtains, pelmets and screens, blinds are very adaptable; they work well with a range of decorating styles.

The earliest forms of blind were purely functional, made to protect the valuable furnishings and curtains in grand houses from the destructive rays of the sun. The very first blinds were more like screens, with

ABOVE LEFT Roller blinds are a good, plain masculine option for bedrooms. The tan leather pull at the base provides a distinctive finishing touch.

ABOVE RIGHT Roller blinds provide a simple solution to curtaining a bay. They create a flat unobtrusive panel at each window, alleviating the need for several sets of curtains, which take up space and can look cluttered.

a piece of linen or silk fabric stretched over a wooden frame; this was attached to the window and occasionally hinged so that it could be swung back. This form of blind continued well into Regency times. By the eighteenth century, blinds were more sophisticated and were used as window dressings in their own right. A forerunner of the Austrian blind had a simple cording system which pulled a loose curtain up into a simple swag at the top. Made from silks and damasks, these blinds were used on elegant Georgian windows both to add drama and to soften the view.

The mid-eighteenth century saw the birth of the roller blind, when the spring blind was invented. These blinds were often highly decorated with paintings and borders. By the nineteenth century, blinds had become an indispensable part of elaborate window treatments of the time. Fussy festoon blinds that retained their ruched appearance even when let down were very popular.

Little is known of the origins of the Roman blind, but they were also popular during the eighteenth century, although not used as often as the festoon and Austrian blinds.

Venetian blinds made from slats of wood were first recorded in the eighteenth century as screens in hot countries, with slats that could be tilted to filter light, or closed to exclude it completely. During the 1930s and 1950s, Venetian blinds became popular as a clean, modern alternative to curtains. Made from wood, plastic and metal in a variety of colours, finishes and widths, Venetian blinds are still a popular choice for kitchens, conservatories and bathrooms today.

Nowadays, there is such a wide range of blinds available, from roller to Roman, Austrian to festoon, Venetian to split-cane, and even pleated paper, that you can find a style to compliment all types of architecture and to suit any personal taste.

THIS PAGE *White roller blinds make an effective screen for privacy during the day, providing a crisp modern alternative to sheers. The stiffened fabric allows the light to diffuse through without the glare of the sun.*

FLAT BLINDS

A flat blind is probably the most basic form of blind possible, being simply a rectangle of fabric that is hemmed and hung up at the window with hooks. Because it is so simple, producing one does not require great sewing skills, and by using an iron-on hemming web, it can actually be made very quickly without even threading a needle.

As a flat blind has no form of mechanism or cords to raise or lower it, you can be very creative and individual in the way the blind is hung up and pulled away to allow the light through. The quickest method is to punch eyelets in the top corners of the blind and hang it from two hooks; it can then be released from one hook to drape down one side of the window, leaving the glass unobstructed. Alternatively, you can place two eyelets at the base corners of the blind as well: this enables the bottom of the blind to be looped up and hooked over the hooks at the top, a method which leaves the top half of the window still covered. There are many variations on this theme, depending on where you place your eyelets and hooks on the blind. The hooks you choose can be as decorative or plain as you wish, a simple nail being the most basic hook possible.

Another method for hanging the blind would be to make buttonholes along the top edge and attach buttons to the window frame. For sheer fabrics that are to be left covering the window all the time, you could make a channel at the top and bottom of the blind, and thread the top on to a net rod and insert a wooden dowel into the base.

Depending on the type of fabric you use for your blind, a flat blind can look either utilitarian, or stylishly contemporary. In cotton checks and linens a flat blind has a Shaker quality, but because the style is so simple it is perfect for more luxurious fabrics, and could even become a stylish banner on which to display embroideries.

FAR LEFT & LEFT *Flat blinds can be either full length covering the whole window, or half length acting as a screen. This half-length blind (far left) has buttonholes worked along the top edge and buttons stuck to the central bar of the sash window, making a feature of the suspension. Full-length blinds can be unhooked during the day and left to tumble effortlessly down one side.*

BELOW LEFT & RIGHT *For a stylish and yet completely no-sew blind, hems can be stuck in place with an iron-on webbing tape, large eyelets punched into the top corners and the blind suspended at the window from two simple nails. You could develop this idea and add more eyelets to the central and lower points of the blind, giving you plenty of scope for variation when you hook the panel up, away from the glass.*

ABOVE *Look out for unusual objects that make decorative hooks. Here metal cupboard handles have been cleverly used to form chunky hooks in proportion with the large copper eyelets. If you use chrome eyelets, make sure that the hooks match.*

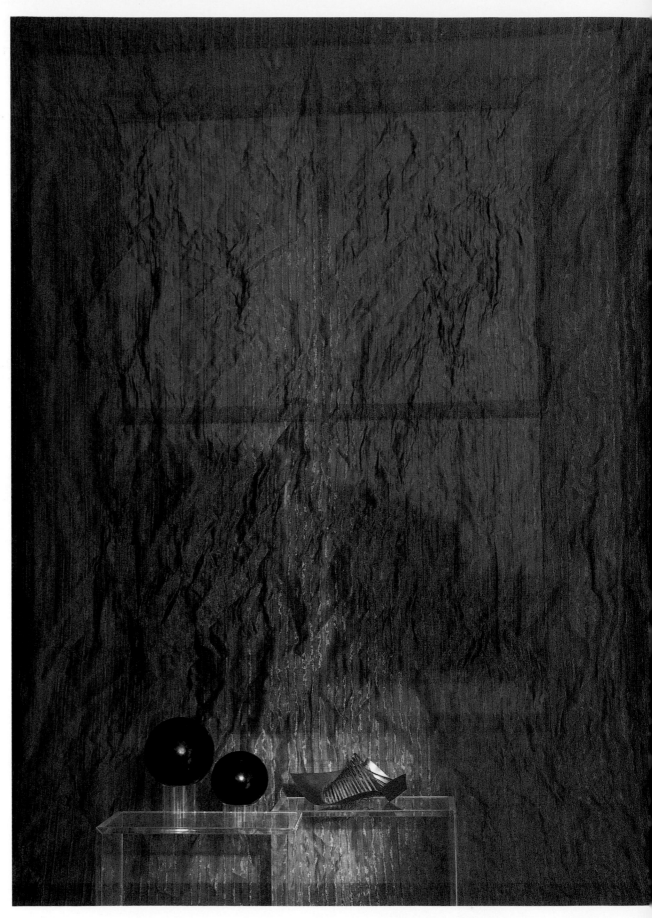

Hooked Panel Blind

The hooked panel blind is modern and minimal and the perfect vehicle for the metallic fabrics available nowadays. Rather like wire-edged ribbon, these new fabrics have fabulous sculptural properties, which allow you to scrunch them up into dramatic shapes. By being hung perfectly flat, this blind allows the fabric to make a statement.

A rectangle of fabric that finishes below the window-sill, with very large eyelets at the heading, makes this the easiest form of blind (see page 144 for instructions on how to make it up). To close the blind, simply hang it on two hooks along the top frame. To open, release the blind from one hook, allowing the fabric to cascade down the other side of the window to the floor. The large eyelets and hooks are one of the main features of this blind. The eyelets are 5cm (2in) in diameter and must be inserted by a specialist company (see Suppliers, page 159), but you can insert smaller ones yourself. The hooks are cupboard door

RIGHT *During the day the blind is unhooked from one corner to cascade in a single swag at the side. A window pole will help you reach the top hook in a tall window.*

FAR LEFT *This blind has a contemporary and minimal appeal, and is the perfect vehicle for showing off an exquisite fabric. At night-time, the flat panel allows the fabric to make a statement in its own right.*

LEFT *The texture and sheen of this striped metallic fabric are really exciting. Like wire-edged ribbon, it can be scrunched up and sculptured in dramatic ways.*

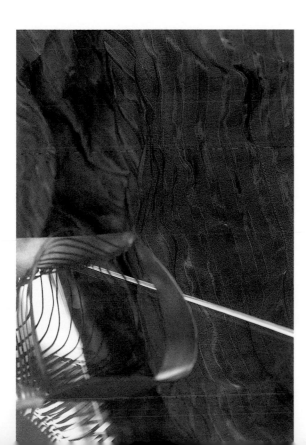

POSSIBLE FABRICS

Metallic fabrics

Embroidered silks

Tapestry

Novelty sheers

Linen

Cotton checks

and stripes

handles, which compliment the proportion of the eyelets perfectly. For the best effect, match the metallic colour of the hooks and eyelets to the fabric.

In practical terms this blind is not really suitable for very tall windows: it would be difficult to reach the hooks at the top. A window pole (a long pole with a hook attached, used for opening high windows and drawing very long curtains in high-ceilinged rooms) could be used. If you cannot find a window pole, screw a hook into one end of a broom handle.

ROLLING BLINDS

'Rolling blinds' is a term which incorporates both roller blinds and more decorative blinds that operate via a cording system. Roller blinds with a spring mechanism are one of the most space-efficient forms of blind. Usually fitted to the top of the window, roller blinds fill the window space with a flat rectangle of fabric when let down, and when rolled up they form a tight cylinder which sits neatly in the space above the window. These blinds are excellent for inward-opening windows and doors, and they are also practical for slanting windows and skylights.

The fabric used for a roller blind must be stiffened for the blind to function properly. This is usually done industrially, and the fabric can be bought in widths wider than normal furnishing fabrics. You can also stiffen ordinary furnishing fabric yourself with a special spray; cotton and linen are best for this process. This stiffening gives the blind a wipe-clean surface, making it a practical option for the kitchen or bathroom.

Roller blinds are usually chosen for their uncluttered plainness, but you can vary the shape of their lower edge, adding trims and embellishing them with paint, to make them decorative as well as functional.

Another form of rolling blind uses a cording system rather like a Roman blind and, as it is not made from pre-stiffened fabric, it has a much softer feel. Although still practical, these blinds are more decorative, with the fabric rolling up on the outside of the blind by means of cords and rings. This type of blind can be made from a variety of fabrics, from a luxurious silk to a simple cotton, as well as from unconventional materials such as split cane or woven hemp, for a more natural feel.

LEFT *In this bright, fun room, roller blinds form blocks of vibrant colour. A plastic strip inserted into the hems of each blind introduces contrasting coloured squares.*

RIGHT *Roller blinds echo the simplicity of this bedroom, with its smooth clean surfaces and geometric shapes. The blinds are neat and unobtrusive, adding plain blocks of colour that tie in with the other elements of this natural colour scheme.*

RIGHT *This roll-down blind covering the lower half of a large arched window provides some privacy. Made from cotton voile, it gently swags, with the help of the cords, as it softly rolls up on the outside.*

BELOW *The operating cords, which loop around on to the face of the blind, are an integral feature of this simple design.*

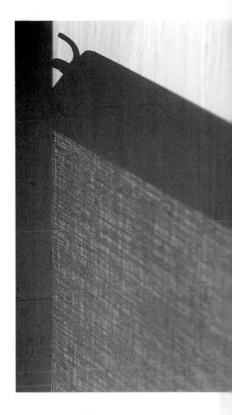

LEFT & RIGHT *A spring-loaded roller blind can be used as a screen in an unconventional way. Fixing it to the windowsill allows it to be pulled upwards, shielding out the sun, while hooks screwed at various heights to the side of the frame hold it in place.*

Roll-up & Roll-down Blinds

Roller blinds are a good choice for a clean, minimal design and have specific practical applications. Because this window was especially awkward, in being tall and having an arched top, a roller blind was set halfway up the window. When unrolled, the blind offers privacy both at night and during the daytime and, as the glazed top section always remains uncovered, allows the daylight into the room.

On first inspection the two blinds featured here look the same; however, they are made and operated in distinctly different ways (see page 145 for making up instructions). The roll-down blind is made from a very lightweight polyester/cotton voile and has a much softer feel. With the help of its cords it gently swags as it rolls up on the outside. The blind never unwinds completely, so when it is fully extended it still has a roll of fabric at the bottom which helps with the momentum. The top of the blind is fixed to a wooden batten attached to the frame, from which the cords are fastened, as they would be on a Roman blind.

The roll-up blind is a spring-loaded roller blind, fixed to the base of the window instead of the top. Much firmer and flatter than the roll-down blind, this blind is made from stiffened cotton fabric. It is pulled up by hand and held in place by hooks, over which the top lath is secured. Hooks can be set at different hieghts on each side of the window to allow the blind to be pulled up to a range of set points. When the blind is not in use, it rolls back very neatly on to the window-sill, leaving the window totally clear.

POSSIBLE FABRICS

Spring loaded blind:

Firm crisp cottons

Linen

Corded blind:

Cotton voile

Soft linens, silks

ABOVE *These unusual arched French windows have been artfully treated with four soft linen Roman blinds, suspended high above the window. As the blinds are unlined, the light passing through them reveals the beautiful arch at the top.*

ROMAN BLINDS

More formal than a roller blind, a Roman blind – with its classic lines – is also more sophisticated. Although, when fully extended, it sits flat against the window and needs little more fabric than a roller blind, a Roman blind has added interest as it is raised – a series of crisp, horizontal folds. To keep the folds in place, the fabric is usually supported by dowels or rods contained in pockets on the reverse of the blind. The blind is lowered and raised by cords threaded through a series of rings stitched to the rod pockets.

The fabric used for making Roman blinds does not need to be stiffened as it would for a roller blind. If left unlined, Roman blinds will gently filter daylight, providing a sophisticated way to diffuse light. When lined or interlined, Roman blinds keep out the cold, and if lined with blackout, they will totally obscure the light, making them perfect for a bedroom.

Roman blinds are architectural in character, and therefore work best with non-patterned fabrics, either plain or striped. Using flat colour can create a bold graphic impact which can be further heightened by attaching contrast borders to the edges. But the effect should still remain free from fussiness. To look chic, Roman blinds should be beautifully made; when the blind is down with the light behind it, all seams and turnings will be visible, unless the blind is blackout lined, so they need to be neat.

Roman blinds can be used on their own, with curtains, or stacked behind a pelmet; they can hang inside or outside the window recess. Roman blinds can be as long as your fabric allows. If wider than 1.5m (5ft) they become unwieldy and should be professionally made as they can sag in the middle. In this instance it is better to divide the window into sections and make a separate blind for each section.

THIS PAGE *A practical, no-fuss choice for a study, this cream-coloured Roman blind in the centre section of the bay forms a smart design feature, as well as lifting and brightening the whole room.*

Studded Leather Blind

This smart leather Roman blind, with its plain square studs, has a very unfussy, masculine feel, making it ideal for a study, or gentleman's dressing room. It looks great when teamed with leather armchairs and books. Roman blinds are functional and simple to operate; men hate curtains that they have to fiddle with.

The blind is fitted into an alcove or recess and, when lowered, it covers the whole window area as a flat leather panel (see page 146 for instructions on making it up). As it can block out the daylight completely, the panel creates a cosy atmosphere. As skins and hides naturally come in varying shapes and sizes, and any joins in the panel will spoil the overall effect of the blind you will be limited to working only on very small windows if you use real leather. Using a

RIGHT Warm tan leather makes an ideal Roman blind for a study or library and blends well with the leather accessories and furniture associated with these rooms.

FAR LEFT & BELOW The blind is attached to its support with decorative studs, echoing studded leather furniture. When lowered, it forms a flat leather panel which gives total black-out, creating a warm cosy glow under artificial lighting. Making this blind needs little sewing skill, as its hems are glued in place.

POSSIBLE FABRICS

Fake leather

Real leather

Mock suede

Canvas

Cotton drill

Denim

mock leather or suede fabric is therefore more practical, and there are some extremely good fakes available these days. Even so, this blind is still best reserved for smaller windows with sills, rather than full-length windows.

Square studs, with an iodized finish, have been used to fasten the blind to the timber support at the top. Another good choice, depending on your window fittings, would be brass studs. However, try to avoid using chrome or ornate studs. In keeping with the plain look of the blind, it has no visible stitching. The side hems are glued in place. The rods slip into pockets formed at the back of the blind, and the cleat is fastened high up the wall so none of the cording shows on the front.

LEFT *This soft Roman blind has no rods in the back, so the fabric concertinas randomly as the blind is raised. The smart brass cleat holding the cords adds a stylish finishing touch.*

BELOW LEFT & RIGHT *When fully extended, these delicate Roman blinds look like flat panel blinds, but with cords and rings attached, they are easily raised, forming soft swags along their base. These blinds are a good choice for French windows as they are unobtrusive and, when raised, allow for clear access.*

Bay Window Blinds

By ensuring that the window treatment does not detract from the rest of the room, and by maintaining a clean simple look, the effect achieved is reminiscent of an American clapperboard house. Although shown here at French windows, soft white blinds work equally well on tall sash windows, but less so on wider landscape styles. Landscape-shaped windows are better suited by conventional Roman blinds.

These blinds are unlined Roman blinds. Although rods are normally inserted to keep the blind rigid and square when raised and lowered, they are omitted here so the blinds swag down at the centre, creating a more informal feel. They can be raised or lowered by cords secured to a brass cleat at the side.

These floor-to-ceiling blinds are made in a lightweight cotton lawn, which does not block out the light but which allows for privacy during the day. If you wish to hang these blinds in a bedroom, use them in conjunction with a blackout roller blind which can be hidden out of sight during the daytime.

The blinds are fastened to the top of the window frame with touch-and-close tape, which means that they can be removed quickly and easily for laundering, an important consideration for white curtains. Whether you choose a white or coloured fabric for your blinds, remember to keep the fabric soft and lightweight, so that the blind scrunches up easily when raised; sharp bulky creases would be out of place for this style.

COMBINATIONS

Curtains have only relatively recently assumed a decorative purpose. Previously, keeping cold and damp at bay was a more pressing concern for most households. The first combination window treatments were thus mainly created for practical reasons; for example, a small curtain to screen out the sun would be combined with a shutter for security at night.

As more curtain styles began to appear so did the desire for decoration and by the eighteenth century, with the vogue for elegant neoclassical interiors, the window became an integral part of a room's decoration. Ruched festoon curtains with pelmets were hung over shutters, and tall elegant windows were swathed with combinations of flowing asymmetrical drapes of lightweight silk and muslin, topped with simple valances and loosely folded blinds. By the end of the nineteenth century, the fashion for combining curtain styles was taken to its extreme. In Victorian times, window treatments became rich, grand and excessive, often consisting of heavy swags and tails, outer curtains, inner curtains, sheer curtains and even linen blinds, leaving the room quite gloomy.

There are still practical reasons for combining window treatments. A heavy outer curtain provides warmth and privacy at night; a sheer inner curtain filters light and provides privacy during the day, while a blind can be pulled down to shield out glare. The trick is not to use them to excess as they were in the past. Combining window treatments offers you the opportunity to exploit contrasts between styles, fabric textures, colours, prints and degrees of transparency. It also allows you to add to an already existing window treatment to create a totally new look.

The success of combining styles can depend on using the different elements in unusual ways, such as a free-standing screen with a Roman blind. Curtains can be used in combinations as a softening element

LEFT & ABOVE *Combining curtains with blinds is both practical and aesthetically pleasing. Blinds are an obvious choice for a bay window, but adding a set of dress curtains outside the bay softens the lines of both the window and the blinds. A blind can also be added to a set of working curtains for extra black-out and thermal properties, while curtains, hung high above a small window, can be used to adjust its proportions.*

for blinds or shutters. These can be working curtains or just dress curtains, whether formally arranged drapes or an unstructured simple length of fabric coiled softly over a pole to cascade down at the sides. Delicate sheers can be hung in front of blackout blinds for a bedroom; alternatively, a sheer blind looks stunning hung behind an opaque curtain.

Window treatments can also be combined for flexibility through the seasons, allowing for different looks throughout the year. Lined or interlined curtains when hung from a pelmet keep out draughts in the winter months; these can be combined with a blind or simple unlined curtains which will provide privacy and act as a sun shield during the summer. Bear in mind, though, that several treatments at the same window will complicate the fitting details.

When using a combination of styles, it is exciting to use a variety of fabric textures and prints, although to work successfully this does need careful thought.

Whole pieces in the arrangement can be made in different fabrics, or you can simply vary details, such as edgings, borders and trims, to pull the whole look together. Combinations of textures can produce dramatic results. Enjoy the contrast of translucent sheers with opaque fabrics. As well as the subtle contrast of the textures, sheers hung behind heavier fabrics diffuse light, bringing a dreamy quality to the room. A sheer hung in front of an opaque fabric will not filter light; instead, the opaque fabric acts as a coloured background to enhance the decorative properties of the sheer. When combining patterns, be bold, but do not go for lots of busy prints. Choose stripes and checks and team them with plain fabrics with textural interest. Pick out a colour from the main print and contrast or co-ordinate it, carrying the idea into the trimmings and lining. Experiment with colours; one colour can assume different characteristics depending on the colour it is combined with.

LEFT *Two sets of curtains have been layered here with sheer blinds. The blinds act as sun-screens, while the coffee-coloured curtains, scooped back at the sides in swags, are for decoration only. Privacy is provided by the cream under-curtains, which are closed at night.*

LEFT *A carefully shaped cane blind has been artfully designed for this beautiful arched window. Covering the glazed area, it shows off the fabulous deep architrave to it best advantage. The cane material also allows the light to penetrate, revealing the window frame in the background. The curtains at either side soften the austerity of the blind and correct the visual proportions of the window, which is small in relation to the height of the room.*

LEFT This dainty sheer curtain with its deep French pleat heading has been skilfully teamed with a pretty, checked Roman blind, which screens the window at night.

RIGHT The light casts transient shadows and contrasts of light and shade into the room when you use a sheer fabric with different levels of transparency results in. Scooping the fabric back to one side further enhances this quality, as the sheer stripes dance in varying directions.

Roman Blind & Sheers

POSSIBLE FABRIC COMBINATIONS

Patterned voiles on coloured woven cottons

Lace on silk or chintz

Novelty sheers on linen

Muslin on ticking stripes

This ground-floor bedroom has a modern double-glazed window, which is large and square. To provide privacy in the room at certain times during the day, a beautiful sheer dress curtain is combined with a Roman blind (see page 148 for instructions on making up). This results in a pretty, feminine window solution without being too fussy.

The full-length sheer curtain is made from a fabulous broad-striped sheer fabric, the stripes creating a wonderful effect when scooped back at the side with a narrow tieback. The curtain is fairly full in order to give just the right amount of privacy during the daytime without having to pull down the blind, which is reserved for the night.

Although a triple-pleat heading is a formal type of heading, it seems softer in appearance here because it is made using curtain tape; this is also much quicker than making triple pleats by hand. The curtain is hung from a curtain track and caught at each end so that it remains fixed and does not move along the track when draped over to one side of the window.

The fully-lined Roman blind is fitted into the window recess and pulls down at night to block out the street lighting. The outer edges of the blind are trimmed with a border in contrasting fabric. Both the fabrics used for the blind are echoed in other furnishings in the room, including the chair and the bedding, for a smart, co-ordinated look.

THIS PAGE *Feminine and romantic, this soft, luxurious sheer fabric can be scooped up and swept to one side with the help of a fine loop of fabric, caught around a small silver hook.*

RIGHT *Denim is a tough practical fabric for a child's bedroom and a 'cool' choice for a teenager. The interlined curtain insulates during the winter, and the blind is great for blocking out the light.*

BELOW *Look out for interesting items to use for tiebacks. Here, children's brightly coloured and striped elastic snake belts look really good fun.*

Denim Blind & Curtain

Deciding on window treatments for children's rooms is always difficult, but this idea is great because it grows up with the child. Denim is a really tough and versatile fabric; it is very practical, ideal for a nursery, yet 'cool' enough for a teenager. There are many shades of denim available, from really dark indigo to washed-out and faded pale blue, and all work well when mixed and matched together. Blue denim has a certain ageless quality, but if you would rather opt for other colours, use cotton drill which is a similar weight to denim and has the same blackout quality.

Combining a Roman blind and curtain (see page 150 for instructions on making up) is both practical and decorative, but you don't have to hang both at the same window; at smaller windows it is best to keep the treatment simple, using just a Roman blind. The blind is the main functional piece as it is easy for children to raise up and down, but you can add a dress curtain purely for decoration, or a working interlined curtain to give extra warmth and excellent blackout qualities. The pelmet is used here simply to

RIGHT & BELOW There is plenty of scope with this style for adding funky details. You could cut up old jeans and stitch the pockets to the lower edge of the blind to create storage pockets. Alternatively, print or stencil motifs on to the blind using fabric paint.

POSSIBLE FABRICS

Denim

Cotton drill

Canvas

Ticking

Patchwork fabric

Tartan

Mock suede

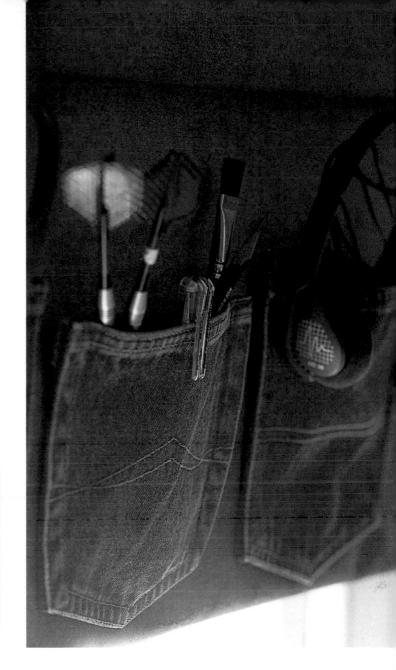

cover the track, but if it is far enough away from the ceiling, it could double up as a display shelf for small toys and treasures.

You can easily add fun details to the blind and curtain. Here, denim pockets from pairs of old jeans have been hand-stitched to the lower edge of the blind; these are perfect for storing little treasures, and easily removable at a later stage. Alternatively, for younger children, you can stencil motifs along the base, or involve your child and let them potato-print a design themselves. Brightly coloured, elasticated snake belts make great tiebacks for the curtain; these can be substituted at a later stage for a leather or chain belt.

LAYERING

Hanging layers of different fabrics together can create exciting window treatments. When choosing fabrics to layer at a window, consider how the light will filter through the material and decide how that will influence the whole effect. Thick, interlined curtains admit very little light and therefore draw attention to the fabric itself. In contrast, unlined curtains made from a silk or light cotton have a slight translucence, while sheer gauzy fabrics have the most transparent qualities of all; they diffuse the light which can create subtle patterns within the room.

For many years, it has been common practice to hang sheer curtains at a window for privacy, combined with heavier outer curtains. Not many people, however, think of placing them the other way around. The appearance of a fabric is changed quite dramatically when covered with a layer of translucent fabric. Strong colours are diffused and weaker ones strengthened. When a 'burnt-out' sheer is hung at a window it emits a delicate tracery of light into a room; if used in overlapping layers it creates interesting shadows, and if hung over plain, unlined, curtains it modifies the underlying colour as the light filters through. If you combine several layers of different coloured sheers you will create glorious stained-glass effects: as the light filters through each overlap produces another colour. This can also affect the mood of a room; pinky shades will create a soft romantic atmosphere while greens provide freshness.

Fabrics do not always have to be combined with sheers, although they probably make the most exciting combinations. Try layering curtains made from different textures, such as smooth silks set against rich velvets or warm woollens, to create rich textural effects. These layers can be pulled back at staggered intervals to hang down straight, or caught back at the sides with tiebacks to reveal the layers beneath. A combined valance and curtain track can be used to hang two different layers in an arrangement, with the addition of a separate pole for a heavier outer drape. Alternatively, layered curtains can be hung from individual tracks screwed to the underside of a pelmet board, while sheer inner panels can be hung from net rods fixed to the window itself. The various headings can then be concealed by a pelmet, or disguised by fabric draped over a pole and hanging down at the sides.

ABOVE City homes with large windows are often overlooked, and privacy – as well as style – becomes a primary consideration. In this modern setting, plain voile curtains are layered with textured wool for a smart, contemporary look.

LEFT *Sheer fabrics are very translucent, but natural linen layered on top adds an interesting contrast. Although opaque, the linen appears sheer with the light behind.*

BELOW *Two soft muslin curtains in different colours have been hung from separate poles, enabling them to be drawn across the window either individually or together to create an interesting looped effect.*

ABOVE *The fine vertical stripes on this sheer fabric are highlighted against the background of taupe silk taffeta as they are twisted and turned back around the transparent glass tieback.*

LEFT *In an unusual twist on a familiar theme, sheer curtains have been hung in front of, rather than beneath, the taffeta curtains.*

Night & Day Curtains

Perfect for tall or French windows, this style of layered curtains creates an air of chic city elegance. Gauzy sheers are hung in front of heavier taffeta curtains from two separate tracks discreetly hidden by a neat box pelmet (see page 152 for instructions on making up). The pelmet can either be covered in matching taffeta fabric or painted to match your walls.

Essentially this novel window treatment is about versatility as there are at least four different ways you can arrange the curtains to create a variety of looks. At night you can draw the taffeta on its own, catching the sheers behind beautiful glass holdbacks at the sides; or to create a delightful, shimmery effect, close both the sheer and the taffeta together. For privacy

RIGHT *The layered fabrics allow you to create a variety of looks. At night, both layers can be closed, with the sheer layer foremost, for a glamorous evening look.*

BELOW LEFT *The effect of the opaque silk seen through the translucent fabric adds new interest to the window treatment and forms the perfect background for the delicate sheer. At night with both layers drawn, the internal lighting creates a delightful shimmery effect, ideal for dining in style.*

during the daytime, draw the sheer curtains across the window and swag the taffeta behind the holdbacks. Alternatively, for maximum light on a dull, grey day, draw back both pairs of curtains together to the sides and arrange them decoratively over the holdbacks. You can also create wonderful effects by using contrasting or co-ordinating colours of fabric. One clever variation is to combine two colours which, when drawn together, form a third. If you use coloured sheers, you will change the tone of light emitted into the room too: blues will give a cool airy feeling, while reds will add warmth to a plain coloured room.

Using a striped or textured sheer for the top curtain will give extra movement to the window treatment. Whatever fabric you choose, remember to keep the overall effect simple.

POSSIBLE FABRIC COMBINATIONS

Ornamental voile on silk taffeta

Organza on silk velvet

Lace on damask

Muslin on cotton weaves

Embroidered tulle on shot-silk dupion

SCREENS
& SHUTTERS

Shutters are usually permanently fixed to windows or doors, although they can be folded or swung out of the way, whereas a screen is either freestanding or temporarily placed across the window as a covering. Like curtains and blinds, screens and shutters help to insulate a room, reduce noise and provide privacy. Shutters are an important asset in the right room. Not only do they look smart when folded back at each side of the window, allowing in maximum light, but they can keep out excess light when necessary.

Freestanding screens are wonderfully versatile pieces of furniture. They can be used to divide up a room space, act decoratively as a backdrop to a piece of furniture, hide away clutter, or provide privacy at a window. The Victorians were great believers in screens in their homes, and used them extensively both in the drawing room and the bedroom. You can still find antique screens, beautifully lacquered,

painted or covered in pretty fabrics. It is a fairly easy task to replace worn-out fabric on an old screen, provided the wooden framework is still sound.

Shutters also make a particularly attractive architectural feature when fixed to the outside of the window. Louvred shutters also look extremely graceful on French windows as a sun-screen, allowing the light to slant through at an angle. The shutters that are popular today, however, are not the exterior kind, but interior – or plantation – shutters with accordion hinges. Most have fine louvres, but they can also be made from solid wooden panels; from fabric stretched between battens to give a light airy interior; or even from heavier fabrics hung flat rather like a banner.

Shutters have been around for centuries they were the original form of window covering. In medieval interiors, windows were small and secured at night with simple internal wooden shutters, which were

sometimes decorated. By the end of the seventeenth century, when the sash window was invented and glass quality improved, tiered (where different sections could be closed at different times) and paired interior shutters gave way to more refined folding shutters, which fitted neatly into a recess in the window embrasure. In grander houses, these shutters were decorated with carved and moulded panels to blend in with the rest of the room, with the face panels sometimes ornately painted. Not all windows had a recess; instead, they were offset with a classical architrave. Screens were often installed at these windows to cut out the sun's glare. Consisting of a simple wooden frame attached to the window over which was stretched a piece of linen or silk, these screens remained popular throughout the eighteenth century. They were sometimes hinged to allow them to swing clear of the window when not required.

In America and European countries, painted shutters were used on simple houses from the eighteenth century onwards, dispensing with any need for curtains. These shutters not only provided excellent security, they kept the interior of the house cool from the heat of the midday sun, and insulated it against winter chills. In Middle Eastern countries, decorative internal window screens were developed to allow the women of the household to maintain their privacy, while enabling them to view the world from their window. Usually made from intricately carved wood, these screens created a secluded and cool interior.

BELOW *A modern folding shutter has been fixed to an old sash window to create a clever combination of old and new. Based on a traditional Japanese paper screen, the shutter forms a clean and effective method of screening the window.*

THIS PAGE *The windows in this bright white, ultra-modern bathroom have been screened with pairs of opaque glass panels secured at the sides with small chrome hinges. They have been designed to blend perfectly with the shower cubicle and shiny glass surface of the wash basin.*

WINDOW SCREENS

Window screens and shutters provide an uncluttered way to block out an undesirable view, give privacy, or filter out the direct sunlight from a room. Some old houses are lucky enough to still retain their lovely wooden window shutters. These offer the perfect window style, and there is no need to add anything to their architectural elegance. If you require a less minimal look you can combine shutters with curtains, sheers and blinds in many effective ways (see page 79).

Modern shutters come in many forms, and can be made from a wide variety of materials. Wooden louvred shutters can be fixed permanently in place, or hinged to fold away at the sides of the window; these are the perfect choice for a summer house or conservatory where light and air are paramount and where solid shutters would be too heavy. Solid wood-panelled shutters with cut-out designs can have a fresh Scandinavian appeal when painted or colourwashed.

Where natural light is required but the view needs obscuring, wooden-framed screens with sheer fabric or mesh stretched across them, rather like mosquito nets, provide effective coverings that can create subtle decorative effects. Whether fixed permanently to the window, or hinged to swing out of the way, these screens offer the ideal site to display some of the wonderful novelty sheers now available. There is another form of fabric shutter which looks rather like a wall hanging. Suspended from a pole that swings across the window at night, this fabric shutter affords both insulation and privacy. You could use tapestries, embroidered hangings, or even oriental rugs to make a bold statement with this shutter.

Window screens do not have to cover the whole window. They can screen just the bottom portion, allowing light to be admitted during the day, while

ABOVE *With the vast selection of ornamental sheer fabrics available, wonderful window screens can be made by stretching the fabric tightly over a frame. These frames can either be propped up against the window, hinged at the side or slid into tracks at the top and bottom.*

shielding the room from the gazes of passers-by. This effect can be achieved using any of the above shutters, or by using a freestanding screen, which can be placed across the window when required. This type of screen is really a piece of furniture, and whether it is a contemporary design or a beautiful antique, it can be used as a starting point around which to decorate your room.

RIGHT *Made with two different, complementary fabrics, one on the front and one on the back, this shutter can affect both the light and mood in the room.*

LEFT *To define the edges of the fabric shutter, a fine border in contrasting silk has been used on all four sides.*

Green Fabric Shutter

This is a fabric banner that, like a shutter, can be swung across or away from the window (see page 153 for instructions on making up). The beauty of this design is that when the shutter is swung back from the window, it allows maximum light to shine through, yet at night it can create a total blackout. This stylish minimalism is achieved by threading a fabric panel on to a hinged brass curtain rod which is attached to the top of the window frame.

This style works best on doors and French windows where the fabric shutter is not obstructed by a radiator or a wide windowsill beneath. Another important consideration is that you need to have a clear, flat wall to one side of the window to allow the

shutter to lie against it when swung away from the window. Although shown here as a single shutter, this design would work equally well as a pair.

As both sides of the shutter will be visible, unlike curtains, they should both be treated rather like separate wallhangings. This shutter is made from a beautiful double-sided heavyweight silk, which is a different colour on each side to give a subtle mood change to the room. The same effect can be achieved by using a contrasting coloured fabric as a lining. The edges have been bound in a bold contrast silk to produce a frame effect. This shutter is the perfect vehicle for displaying dramatic fabrics, such as those with large motifs – even beautiful pieces of embroidery.

POSSIBLE FABRIC COMBINATIONS
Double-sided silk with silk taffeta trim
Tapestry with cotton sateen
Appliqué and embroideries with heavy silk

THIS PAGE *The fabric shutter is threaded on to a hinged brass rod, which allows it to swing back and forth. It is important to have sufficient wall space to accommodate the open banner.*

THIS PAGE AND FAR RIGHT
*A freestanding screen
is a very versatile option
for covering a window.
This graceful, modern
polypropylene screen with
a maple and polished
aluminium frame, works
rather like a sheer, allowing
the light to filter through.
At night, the Roman blind can
be lowered to create a total
blackout at the window.*

Standing Screen

If you are not over-fond of curtains, but would still like a degree of privacy at your windows, the idea of using a freestanding screen in conjunction with a Roman blind could be the perfect solution. The screen becomes an accessory to the window, and you can choose to position it either totally or halfway across the window, or even to put it to one side when It Is not required. It can be used with both full-length and smaller windows with sills, as well as on its own to shield French windows or a glazed door. The fact that the screen is freestanding not only means that you can move it around to the

> **POSSIBLE FABRIC COMBINATIONS**
>
> *Sheer screen with an opaque blind*
>
> *Wooden screen with an opaque blind or a sheer blind*
>
> *Antique screen with an opaque blind*

LEFT *This Roman blind makes an elegant companion to the freestanding screen. When raised, it folds up neatly with the help of timber rods set into the pockets on the reverse. It has also been lined to give it more density when used at night.*

most desirable position, but also that there is no measuring and fitting involved; the screen can be larger or smaller than the window and it would not make any difference.

The screen is actually a piece of furniture in its own right. As with any other window treatment it should blend in with the rest of the room. The screen featured here is wonderful as it does not totally block out the daylight yet it provides a degree of privacy to the room. Shafts of light pierce the polypropylene panels to let diffused light through, rather like a sheer curtain. It is possible to use all sorts of things as a screen, and even to make your own (see page 154 for instructions on making up). You can hinge together wooden frames covered in a sheer fabric, or use wooden panels, painted medium density fibreboard (MDF), or even garden trellis.

Using a Roman blind in conjunction with the screen means that it can be lowered at night and the screen folded away. The blind is fitted outside the window recess but needs to be kept simple so as not to detract from the screen during the day.

ROOM DIVIDERS

BELOW LEFT The metal roof supports in this modern loft conversion have been used like washing lines: vast sheets of white muslin are draped over the top, creating tent-like room dividers.

BELOW RIGHT A large glazed panel etched with a simple design of squares lets the light refract through at different angles.

Screens offer a simple way to change the proportions and shape of a room, breaking it up into smaller areas without losing the feeling of space. The Japanese are the experts; they have been doing it for years. They use lightweight, wooden-framed screens to separate off eating, sleeping and cooking areas. Throughout the day, the screens can be moved around as the mood dictates to create a different environment. This sort of treatment is perfect for one-room living, such as a bedsit, where you can separate off the different areas with the screen making a room cosier. Screens are also good for hiding clutter, or messy working areas.

For permanently positioned room dividers, roller or Venetian blinds, which can be raised or lowered as the situation dictates, offer a clean and uncluttered modern solution. For a more traditional method, curtains make good room dividers. These can be used where a dividing wall has been knocked through, leaving an archway. As the curtains are seen from both sides, they can be lined with two complementary fabrics to suit each room. A wooden frame with fabric stretched across it and attached to the wall with hinges, enabling it to be swung out or back against the wall as required, would be another permanent solution.

Freestanding screens offer the most versatile and temporary way of screening off an area. These can be solid wood, or simple wooden frames with glass, paper or fabric centres. Screens are fairly easy to make and are a wonderful medium for showing off a special fabric or a piece of work you have created yourself, whether stitched, painted or dyed. A screen can be covered with identical fabrics on both sides, or contrasting fabrics to give you two screens in one. Whether covered in fabric, or made from coloured glass, room dividers offer an eclectic choice.

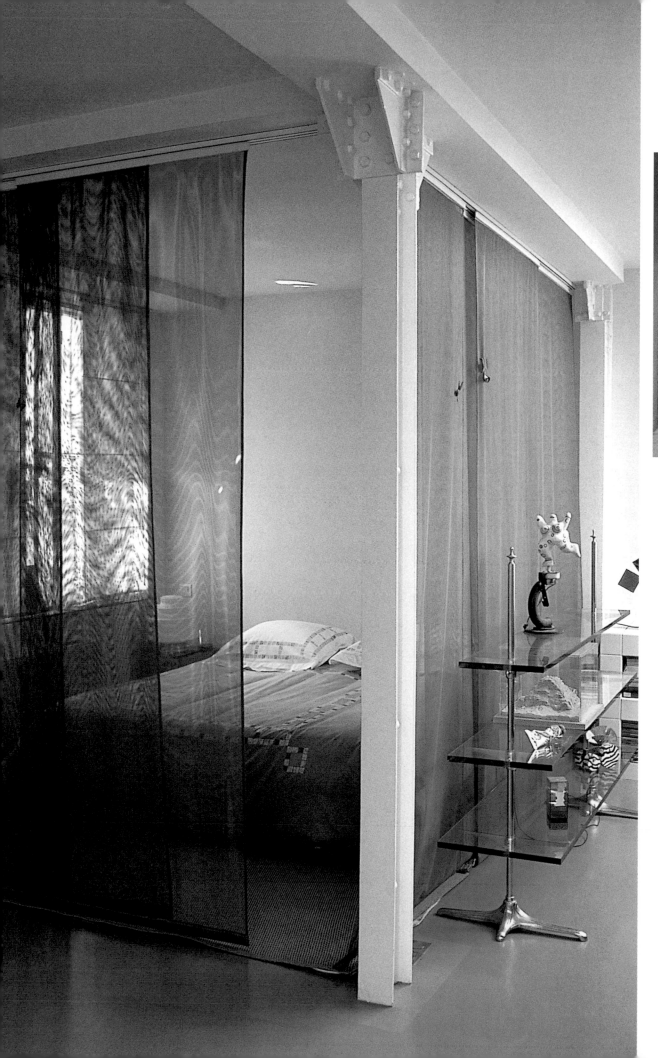

ABOVE *Large, sliding bronze-glass doors prove the perfect room divider for this stylish apartment. When the 'doors' are fully opened, the space opens up into a large reception room; when closed, it forms a more intimate dining area.*

LEFT *The girders and beams in this warehouse conversion have formed a natural frame for the bed. Sheer fabric panels are suspended from the beams, separating the sleeping quarters from the living area.*

ABOVE *Frayed opaque squares of fabric have been woven into this sheer at regular intervals to create interest. Stretched out taut on a frame, both fabric and effect are seen at their best.*

RIGHT *Hinged from a batten on the wall, this screen can be swung out to split the room, or laid back flat against the wall. It would make an ideal room divider for a flat.*

Sheer Door Panel

This door panel is very versatile. It can be used as a French door to give privacy without blocking out any daylight, or as a room divider to separate off different living areas within a room, an idea that is perfect for a studio apartment. Made simply from a wooden rectangular frame with a piece of sheer fabric stretched across it, the panel is hinged to a door frame rather like a mosquito net. Thus it can be opened and closed with the door, while at the same time allowing easy access for cleaning the door windows (see page 156 for instructions on making up). The sheer door panel works both on a single glazed door and, as a pair, on French windows. As a room divider, it can be hinged to a wooden batten fixed to the wall; the panel can be swung back against the wall when not required and opened out only when necessary – in bright, glaring sunlight, for example.

The height of the panel is up to you. It can be the same height as your door, the height of a standing screen, which would cover about two-thirds of the door, or even ceiling height. Likewise, you can decorate the panel frame in any way you choose: you can paint it to match your decor or keep it natural by giving it a natural woodstained finish with varnish or wax; you could even add a door handle to help with opening and closing.

The sheer flat panel is rather like the canvas of a painting but different effects will be possible depending on your fabric choice. There are a great number of beautiful self-coloured, patterned fabrics available, ranging from stripes to prints and bobbly weaves, which will all help to divert attention from an ugly view. Choosing a coloured sheer fabric will affect the light tone in a room, but it would look fabulous with an elaborately decorated frame.

POSSIBLE FABRICS

Novelty sheers

Printed and patterned muslin

Striped voile

Embroidered tulle

Shot organza

Coloured net

BELOW *Decorated sheer fabrics are ideally suited for this screen, as their true beauty can be appreciated in the flat panel. Whether hinged singly or in pairs to the sides of the door, they look like mosquito screens seen in hot countries, and work perfectly for shielding the sun and creating privacy.*

Mesh Screen

Although not strictly speaking a window treatment, this screen is formed in principle like a window blind and serves to some extent the same purpose (see page 157 for instructions on making up). A mesh screen is the perfect choice for a warehouse apartment or for offices, as a means of dividing up a large area without losing the feeling of space. It is also a cheap way of dividing a room without having to get the builders in.

The screen is suspended from the ceiling on chains, so that it hangs to the floor. The screens featured here are made by a specialist blind manufacturer, but they are very easy to make yourself. Choose a mesh-type fabric, which allows the light to pass through; this looks great when you light the areas on each side of the screen differently. Ready-stiffened roller-blind fabric provides the best results, the main consideration to bear in mind is that the fabric is wide enough as you cannot join this type of fabric successfully with seams. If you are unable to find a fabric that is wide enough, make more than one screen and hang them side by side.

For smaller rooms, such as a combined sitting room and dining area, you could adapt this idea and fasten an actual roller blind to the ceiling to create the same effect. This will provide a temporary lightweight divider which can be rolled down when you are home alone and wish to create a snug feel, or raised when you need to open up the room for entertaining.

FAR LEFT & LEFT *Screens allow you to divide a large area without losing the feeling of space, as glimpses of each area are still visible around the screens.*

BELOW *These screens are suspended from wooden battens fixed to the ceiling. Hung decoratively from long chains and hooks, they fall vertically, down to the floor.*

THIS PAGE *These stylish screens are an inexpensive way to divide up large areas. They also allow you flexibility to rearrange and form new spaces within the living area.*

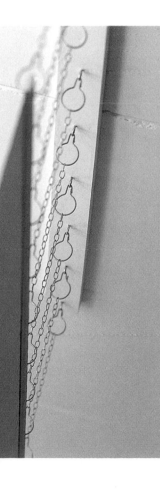

All curtains and blinds can be greatly enhanced by the addition of a few, well-chosen details that emphasize the design of the whole window treatment, whether that be exuberant or restrained.

adding detail

EQUIPMENT & HEADINGS

Having the right tools for the job can make the difference between successful and enjoyable sewing and an evening of frustration. Do not be put off, however, by thinking you need lots of expensive equipment and expert sewing skills to create a stylish window treatment. Many of the projects featured in this book can be stitched by hand, and some achieved without any sewing at all, so you don't even need to own a sewing machine! There are also plenty of sewing aids available that can help you achieve smart and elegant headings without requiring extensive experience.

LEFT *Certain sewing tools and aids will make life much easier and create a more professional finish. Sewing machines are not always necessary but will speed up your work. All you require for window coverings is a basic machine: one that does straight stitching for seams, and zigzag for neatening and buttonholes. Choose the right type of needle and sewing thread for your fabric, and match colours one shade darker to blend in. Probably the most important piece of equipment you will need is bent-handled shears for cutting out; try to go for the best quality you can afford, treat them well and don't use them for cutting paper! For accuracy use a steel tape when measuring, and have plenty of rust-proof stainless-steel pins. Look around a haberdashery department and you'll find lots of things designed to help you achieve a professional finish.*

BELOW *In the past, decorative headings for curtains had to be made by hand; now, however, the easiest method is using one of the many heading tapes available on the market. These tapes have pockets for inserting curtain hooks and draw-cords running through them which, when pulled up, gather the fabric in a decorative way. Instruction booklets produced by the manufacturers will help you to choose the correct tape, and offer tips on applying the tape and the type of hooks and accessories required. Now there are also no-sew versions of some of the basic tapes: these can be ironed on, and used with stick-on touch-and-close tape. Touch-and-close tape is a versatile option for hanging blinds, pelmets and curtains, allowing them to be removed easily.*

ABOVE *As poles are decorative, most pole brackets are face-fixed protruding from the wall, supporting the pole from underneath, but recess brackets are available for more functional poles, allowing you to set them into the window recess. As the pole selection has increased, so too the brackets have become more attractively designed, becoming part of the total look and no longer just playing a functional role.*

RIGHT *With a tension wire, the cable is threaded through a series of brackets screwed to the wall or ceiling.*

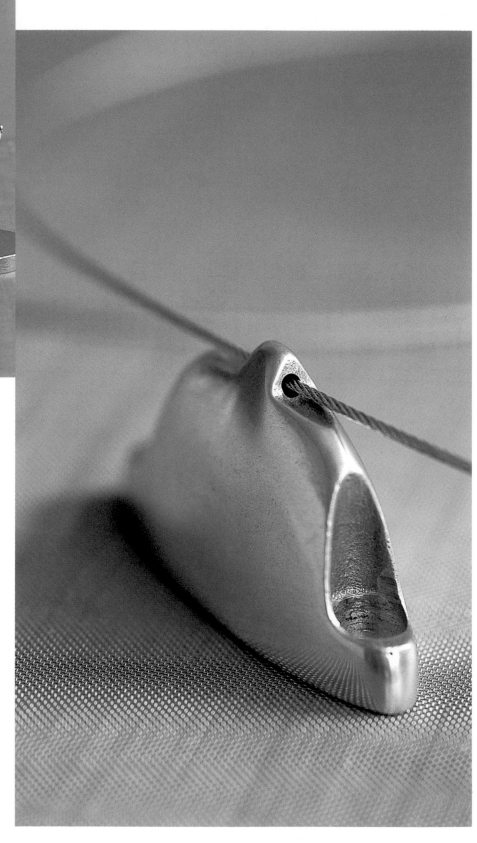

ABOVE LEFT Shiny chrome and stainless-steel poles have a contemporary feel – ideal for a modern room. Available in various diameters, they can be used with rings, clips or ties, and look especially good with a large chrome eyelet heading.

LEFT Modern designers have started to focus on this area. Previously neglected, poles are now produced in an array of new, up-to-date materials. Stainless steel, chrome, resin and tension wires have become popular; their clean finishes work well with modern interiors.

POLES & BRACKETS

Curtain poles serve both a functional and a decorative purpose. They provide the means of support for a pair of curtains, while at the same time they can be draped in swags of fabric, encased by a slotted heading, or used with clips or eyelets to create very differing effects.

Over the past few years, the selection of poles and brackets available has been revolutionized. Traditionally restricted to brass or wood, now you can find anything from stainless steel and chrome, to wrought iron, perspex, and many that combine wood, metal and paint effects. You can also get poles that go around corners now, extending the number of locations where poles and brackets can be used. Tension wire has been another introduction; this very modern look can be shaped to fit any window alcove, or even stretched around an entire room.

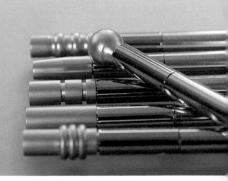

ABOVE A selection of decorative metal sheaths that slip over the ends of the pole – designed as simple but effective finials for the ends of these metal poles.

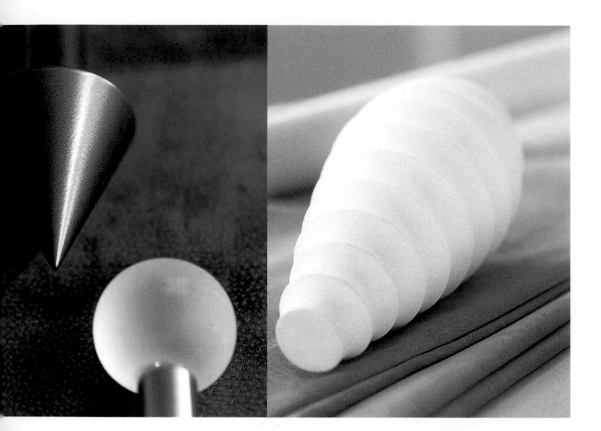

FAR LEFT & LEFT *Resin and metal can be carved into stylish modern finials, making sleek and graphic shapes with either light-reflective or translucent properties.*

BELOW *Gone are the days of the plain wooden knob. These ethnic-looking finials have been carved from dark wood and attached to a metal pole – for a contemporary look. Clear, coloured or decorated glass balls, rather like paperweights, make brilliant finials as they reflect and sparkle in both natural and artificial light.*

FINIALS

Finials are the decorative 'stops' that fasten on to each end of a curtain pole. They play an important role in the design of a window treatment, as they make a final statement. Simple finials can be used with busily styled curtains, while more elaborate ones look effective with simpler, plain curtains.

Today, there are a huge variety of designs available on the market, ranging from the simple contemporary wrought iron finial, shaped into a shepherd's crook, through to designs made in brass and other metals, wood, resin, glass and porcelain. You could also make your own finials by covering wooden ones in fabric, or design your own unique wire or leather finials.

ABOVE *Modern designers have gone into a frenzy about developing new and interesting finial styles. From simple frosted-glass balls to lumpy light-bulb shapes, glass looks wonderful high up as it catches the light. In metal there are basic moulded designs, ranging from solid polished balls and cylinders, to more intricate styles using wrapped wire or cable to resemble an old-fashioned thread bobbin.*

LEFT *An intricate cage has been made from twisted wire to house the two-toned glass beads for this finial.*

CLIPS, HOOKS & RINGS

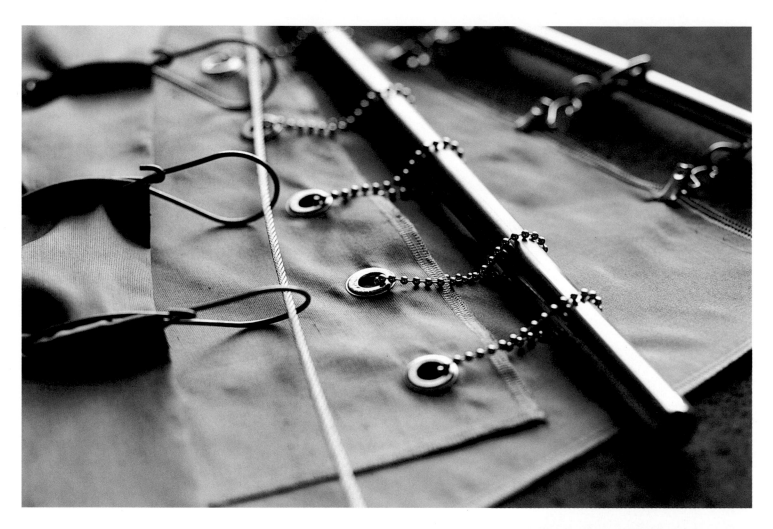

At one time curtain rings were only made from wood; in recent years, however, new and more stylish ways of suspending curtains and blinds from their poles or wires have been developed. With the arrival of these new attachments, there has been a move away from traditional curtain headings to flatter plainer styles that use the new clips, hooks and rings to form decorative headings themselves. With no-sew options like clip-on rings or tabs, peg-like clips, twisted wires and eyelets, anybody can achieve simple yet chic window coverings.

ABOVE & RIGHT *Ready-made no-sew options include funky twisted wires that pinch the fabric in place; rings with clips to grip the fabric; or simple eyelets threaded on to cable. You could make your own budget alternative by threading chrome ball-chain paper fasteners through eyelets.*

FAR LEFT *The choice of rings can be bewildering. Some are fitted with inner nylon rings to help them glide better; others have peg-like clips attached to the base; some have linked rings to take a hook; while others are spring-loaded to grip the fabric.*

LEFT *Tension wires are the newest form of suspension; with their brackets they resemble somewhat the rigging on a yacht. A variety of wire rings, clips and hooks are available for use with these wires.*

RIGHT *The range of materials used for suspension is now extensive – from leather tabs and wooden rings to polished chains, and iodized metal which creates intriguing effects.*

FAR RIGHT *For metal poles you can choose from a selection of rings, clips and hooks. Choose from simple plain rings, decorative twin rings held together at the base, or wire hooks looped around the pole.*

TIEBACKS & TASSELS

Although tiebacks are not an essential element in curtain design, and simple loose-hanging curtains can look wonderful, adding a tieback will instantly alter the look and effect of a curtain. By scooping back the fabric at any point along its length, tiebacks and holdbacks give a curtain a great new shape, often creating the illusion of fullness at the same time. There is a wide variety of tiebacks available – some wrap, some tie, some loop and hook – and you don't need to spend a vast amount of money to buy something exciting; you could even try using candlesticks as holdbacks. Be practical when choosing your tiebacks. Make sure that you can fix them easily to the wall and, once in position, that they will be hidden somehow when not in use.

ABOVE AND RIGHT
Cord tiebacks are often embellished with tassels. When made from twisted silky yarns these form sumptuous tassels with a pearly sheen. Alternatively, matt materials, such as cotton, leather and suede, can be used to create tassels with a very different feel.

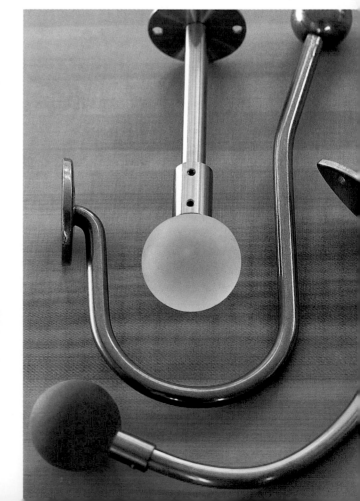

LEFT *In the past, brackets were either carved in wood or cast in brass. Nowadays, they are made from other metals in various designs. The simplest form is a plain U-shaped loop, which can be decorated in some way at the end. Ombras look rather like cloak pegs, consisting of a short shaft, ending in a disk or knob at the end. Traditionally these disks were carved rosettes or similar circular motifs. Thankfully, today there are many other options, like the stylish glass ball shown here.*

ABOVE LEFT & RIGHT *Feathers were the inspiration behind these tiebacks. The amazing brackets have been hand-blown in glass with a feather-like design, to form elegant curved hooks. They are attached to the wall with metal bosses which thread on to a wall plate. The black tieback has a pair of large silky tassels, formed from raven black feathers, bound on to a silky cord. This tieback would form a stunning and dramatic contrast to a plain natural-coloured curtain.*

making up

Basic techniques for measuring, cutting and stitching, together with detailed step-by-step instructions, to show you how to make up twenty different window treatments.

MEASURING UP

It is best to have all your poles, tracks and fittings in place before you begin to measure – including carpets for full-length curtains. For accuracy, use a long, retractable steel tape measure and ask someone to help you measure large windows.

Take the finished length measurement a few times across the window width, as floors can sometimes be uneven, and check, by measuring the width at both the top and the bottom, whether your window is true. Take your time when measuring up. It is important to get the measuring correct to avoid expensive mistakes when buying and cutting out your fabric. Check every measurement twice, but don't worry unduly, because small measuring mistakes can usually be rectified.

CURTAINS

POSITIONING CURTAIN TRACKS AND POLES

Both tracks and poles come in a large range of lengths, weights and types of finish for different end uses and curtain weights. Usually they come packaged with all the necessary fixings, together with full fitting instructions.

• Tracks can be fixed directly to the wall or ceiling, but if the plaster is not too good, it may be better to face-fix them to a wooden batten screwed to the wall. Poles are usually face-fixed by brackets that protrude from the wall, but they can also be set into a window recess using special recess brackets.

• For an exposed or visible pole or track, you should ideally fix them about 15cm (6in) above the top of the window; allow the same distance at each side of the window to the end of the track, or last ring on the pole beyond the supporting brackets (measurement A in diagram **1A**).

• A track hidden by a pelmet needs to be screwed to the underside of a pelmet board (see page 121). The pelmet board should be the same length as the curtain track (measurement A), plus 5cm (2in), and fitted in the same position above the window as an exposed track.

MEASURING FOR CURTAINS

There are two basic measurements that you will need to know before you can begin to estimate how much fabric you will need:

1A

1B

1 The length of the curtain track or pole (measurement A), plus the length of the overlap arms at the centre if your track has them.

2 The length of the curtain from the track to the window-sill (measurement B), or the floor (measurement C).

Length

• For curtains hung from a track screwed to a pelmet board, measure the finished length from the underside of the board. Then work out the hook drop. This will depend on the type of heading tape and curtain track you are using. If you are not sure, hang a piece of the heading tape from the track to measure the clearance between the top edge and base of the board.

• For curtains hung from an exposed track, you will need to work out where the heading tape will finish in relation to your track. If you are not sure, hook a piece of the heading tape on to your track and measure down from the top of your tape.

• For curtains hung from a pole, measure the length from the base of a curtain ring.

• For curtains threaded on to a pole, add 3cm (1¼in) above the pole to allow for eyelets.

• For sill-length curtains, and if your window-sill protrudes a long way, deduct 1cm (⅜in) from measurement B (see diagram **1A**); this will allow for the curtains to hang clear. If possible, try to make the curtains hang just below the sill, as this looks much more attractive. To do this, add 5–10cm (2–4in) to measurement B.

• For full-length curtains, deduct 1cm (⅜in) from measurement C (see diagram **1A**) for clearance. If you want them to drape on the floor, add 5–20cm (2–8in) to the finished length, depending on taste.

MEASURING FOR BOX PELMETS

The depth of the pelmet should be in proportion to the length of your curtains. A plain straight pelmet is usually one-eighth of the curtain drop, although a shaped pelmet may drop lower at the sides.

The width of the pelmet needs to be the length of your pelmet board along the front edge (see page 121), which is measurement A plus 5cm (2in), and then plus the sides of the pelmet board (measurement D).

MEASURING FOR TIEBACKS

Measure around the curtain at the chosen height, making sure that the tieback will not crush the fabric or hang away too loosely from the curtain's leading edge. Make a template or pattern for your tieback shape; this will help you to work out how much fabric you will need.

BLINDS

Blinds can be fixed either inside or outside the window recess. The former is neater for Roman and roller blinds, but it will block out some daylight and can obstruct the window from opening. Blinds hung outside give more flexibility as regards size and can make a window appear larger.

POSITIONING BLIND SUPPORTS

• A recess-fixed Roman blind is fixed in place with a timber support (see opposite) screwed to the top of the recess (measurement E).

• For a recess-fixed roller blind, the brackets need to be fitted about 3cm (1¼in) in from the top of the recess to allow the blind room to roll up. The length of the roller blind pole from the end of the square pin to the end of the round pin is the width of the recess (measurement E) minus 5mm (¼in).

• For face-fixed Roman blinds, the timber support is screwed to the wall with little brackets (see page 122). The support should be positioned 12cm (5in) above the window and with the same distance each side of the window (measurement F).

MEASURING FOR BLINDS

For the finished length of a recess-fixed blind, measure from the top of the timber support or roller to the window-sill (measurement G; see diagram **1B**). The finished width is the width of the recess (measurement E), minus 2cm (¾in), so that the blinds do not touch the sides of the window.

For the finished length of a face-fixed blind, measure from the top of the timber support or roller down to 5cm (2in) below the window-sill (measurement H). However, if your sill projects a long way, subtract 1cm (⅜in) from the length for the blind to hang just clear of it.

The finished width for a Roman blind is the length of the timber support (measurement F) plus 1.5cm (⅝in). For a roller blind it is the length of the pole including metal caps and pins, minus 3cm (1¼in) for clearance.

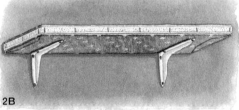

2A

2B

MAKING & FIXING A PELMET BOARD

A pelmet board needs to be made from timber that does not bend, such as pine or plywood, approximately 2–2.5cm (¾–1in) thick.

1 Cut the board 12–30cm (5–12in) deep, depending on your project, so that it projects far enough beyond the track to allow the curtains to move freely behind. The length of the board should be the same as the curtain track plus 2.5cm (1in) at each end, 5cm (2in) in total.

2 Cover the board with fabric (**2A**); attach this to the underside with **staples** or spray adhesive. Alternatively, you might want to paint the pelmet board to match your walls or window frame.

3 Staple the hook side of a length of touch-and-close tape to the narrow sides, and front edges of the pelmet board. This is to attach the pelmet.

4 Using angle brackets, attach the board to the wall, about 15cm (6in) above the top of the window; it should look like a shelf above the window (**2B**). Screw your curtain track or tracks to the underside of the board, if required. These should be positioned centrally down the board, so the curtains can be drawn easily when the pelmet is in place.

MAKING AND FIXING A TIMBER ROMAN BLIND SUPPORT

The support should be made from 5 x 2.5cm (2 x 1in) timber covered in fabric, to match the blind, or painted to match the wall or window frame.

1 Cut the support to the finished width of the blind less 1.5cm (⅝in) for a face-fixed blind and 3cm (1¼in) for a recess blind. With recess blinds the support is usually fixed directly to the window recess; you may need small angle brackets.

2 For a recess-fixed blind, drill two holes 15cm (6in) in from each end on the wide side of the timber, making sure that they do not interfere with the cording screw eye positions (see individual projects). Cover the timber with fabric and staple or glue in place, or paint to match your décor.

3 Staple the hook side of a length of touch-and-close tape to one of the long narrow sides of the support (**3A**). For a face-fixed blind without a pelmet at the top, fix the hook side of the touch-and-close tape to the top of the timber support. This will hide the blind machinery from view. Remember, though, to allow for the tape at the top when measuring up for the finished blind length.

4 Using a bradawl, mark the positions of the cording screw eyes on the timber support.

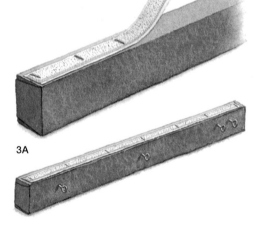

3A

3B

3C

3D

Line them up with the rows of cording rings on the blind and secure in place. Screw an extra eye 2.5cm (1in) in from one end of the support, at the cord operating end (**3B**).

5 For a recess-fixed blind, pierce the fabric covering the support holes and screw the support to the frame (**3C**) in the right position. For a face-fixed blind, screw small angle brackets to the underside of each end of the support. Drill fixing holes in the wall and screw the brackets in place, approximately 12cm (5in) above the window (**3D**).

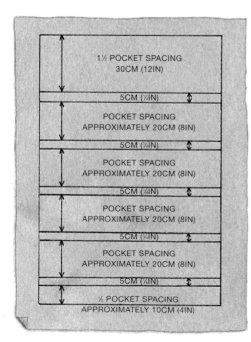

1½ POCKET SPACING
30CM (12IN)

5CM (¼IN)

POCKET SPACING
APPROXIMATELY 20CM (8IN)

5CM (¼IN)

POCKET SPACING
APPROXIMATELY 20CM (8IN)

5CM (¼IN)

POCKET SPACING
APPROXIMATELY 20CM (8IN)

5CM (¼IN)

POCKET SPACING
APPROXIMATELY 20CM (8IN)

5CM (¼IN)

½ POCKET SPACING
APPROXIMATELY 10CM (4IN)

4A

ESTIMATING FABRIC QUANTITIES

Once you have fitted your tracks, poles, timber supports and pelmet boards in place, and have measured up the window size, you are in a position to work out how much fabric to buy. Some of the projects have special information on hems, etc., relating to that particular style, so check and then follow the instructions below.

CURTAINS

Measure your window (see page 120) to establish the finished width and length of the curtains.

Main fabric

To calculate how many fabric widths you need, multiply the length of the curtain track by the fabric fullness required (see the individual projects). Divide this by the width of your chosen fabric and then round up the total to the nearest fabric width.

Always place a full width at the leading edges. So, if you are making a pair of curtains, and an odd number of fabric widths is needed, cut the odd width in half lengthways and join each half-width on the outer edges of each curtain.

To calculate the total quantity of fabric required, add the appropriate hem allowances given with each project. (If your curtains are to have bound hems or borders you may have to subtract from the curtain length, not add on.) Multiply this final drop measurement by the number of widths you previously calculated, to get the final amount.

If your chosen fabric has a pattern repeat, add one full pattern repeat per fabric width required after the first width. For example, a curtain with four widths will need three repeats added to the total.

Lining and interlining

Choose a lining and interlining the same width as your fabric, so that you can match the seams. Work out the amounts in the same way as for the main fabric, but you need only add 18cm (7in) for hem allowances on the lining fabric; there is no need to allow for fabric repeats.

SHEERS

Sheer fabrics often come in very wide widths of 3m (3¼yd) or more, so there may be no need to join widths. Simply add 20cm (8in) to the curtain length for hems at the top and base (unless the fabric is ready-weighted, then add only 7.5cm [3in] for a top hem), and multiply the width by the fabric fullness required. For narrower fabric that has to be joined, work out the fabric as for the lined curtains above. If your sheer fabric is not long enough for the drop, you will have to join an extra piece to the lower edge of the curtain. If this is the case, make a feature of the join, by forming it into a decorative tuck, or a bold flat fell seam (see page 128). Allow for the extra piece to be stitched to the lower edge, and include a wide 4cm (1½in) seam allowance for making the special join.

PELMETS

To calculate the amount of fabric needed for the pelmet, divide the width of the finished pelmet (including returns) by the width of your fabric, and allow for a hem allowance of 2.5cm (1in) all round. Again a full fabric width should be placed centrally along the pelmet, with any part-widths at each side. Work out the lining and interlining quantities in the same way, choosing a lining and interlining the same width as your fabric.

LINED ROMAN BLINDS

Measure your window as shown on page 120, to find the finished width and length of the blind.

Main fabric

Add 10cm (4in) to the finished width and length of the blind for hem allowances. If you need more than one width of fabric for your blind, cut the extra width in half lengthways and join each piece to the outer edges of the blind.

Lining

Work out the spacing for the rod pockets. For an average blind, allow 10cm (4in) between the lowest dowel and the hem edge (a half-pocket spacing), unless otherwise specified. Place the top pocket 30cm (12in) from the top edge; space the remaining pockets evenly between, approximately 20cm (8in) apart (a full-pocket spacing), depending on the size of the window (see **4A**).

Once you have worked out the rod pocket spacing, you can estimate the lining quantity. Allow for one piece to finish the final width of the blind if you need more than one width of fabric (see Main fabric). For the length, allow the finished depth of the blind, plus 5cm (2in) per rod pocket and 10cm (4in) for a top-edge allowance.

UNLINED ROMAN BLINDS

Measure your window as shown on page 120, to find the finished width and length, then on a piece of paper work out the spacing for the rod pockets, as described for the lining of a lined Roman blind.

Once you have worked out the spacing, you can estimate the fabric quantity. Allow for one piece to finish the final width of the blind, plus the stated hem allowance for the individual project. If you need more than one width of fabric, see the Main fabric section for the Lined Roman blind and join widths with flat fell seams (see page 128). For the length, allow the finished depth of the blind, plus 5cm (2in) for each rod pocket and the stated hem allowances for the individual project.

CUTTING OUT

The most important thing you need is a sharp pair of cutting shears. Before you start to cut, however, check the whole length of the fabric for fabric faults, and double check your fabric calculations to make sure that you have added on the amounts required for hem allowances and pattern repeats. Iron out any creases and cut out on a flat surface.

1 So that the curtain or blind will hang well, each fabric drop needs to be cut off square. With a loosely woven fabric, you can pull a crossways thread from the fabric width and use the channel formed by the withdrawn thread as a cutting line (**5A**). With other fabrics, use a set square and a long ruler to draw a line across the width of the fabric at right angles to the selvedge (**5B**).

2 Check which is the base edge of the fabric and make sure this is cut square. Sometimes patterns are not always printed straight on the grain. When this occurs, follow the pattern and not the grain when you cut; as long as the pattern is no more than 5cm (2in) out of alignment, it should not cause a problem. Mark the base by snipping off the corner, then measure up from the base edge and cut off your first curtain length (or drop).

3 Cut out the remaining curtain lengths required, taking care to match any pattern repeats on each length. Mark the base edge of each piece by snipping off the corner, as before.

4 If you need to cut a curtain length into two half-widths, fold it in half lengthways matching the selvedges and carefully cut down the fold.

5 Trim away the selvedges from each curtain length. This tightly woven edge can sometimes cause seams to pucker when pressed flat.

JOINING FABRIC WIDTHS

On plain fabrics, you can join widths with plain straight seams, French seams or flat fell seams (see page 128), depending on the type of fabric and the project. It is best to stitch all your seams in the same direction (from base to top), matching the base marks to ensure that the pile, shading and patterns run the same way on all the lengths.

On patterned fabrics, match the pattern before stitching. Tack the layers together with ladder stitch (see page 129), open out the seam turnings, and stitch together as usual.

CURTAIN AND BLIND BASICS

MAKING UNLINED CURTAINS

Unlined curtains can provide a soft translucent finish to a window, allowing the daylight to filter through the fabric. They are an excellent project for the novice curtain-maker, as good results can be achieved very easily by hand or machine. It is advisable to pre-wash the fabric and heading tapes before making them up, to avoid any shrinkage. Even if the fabric demands dry-cleaning, wash the tapes. Pencil-pleat, gathered and slot headings are all appropriate headings for unlined curtains.

1 Cut out the required number of fabric drops and join any widths together using French seams (see page 127) on lightweight fabrics and flat fell seams (see page 128) for heavier fabrics.

2 Press a double 1.5cm (⅝in) hem along the side edges of the fabric and machine stitch in place (**6A**). Use a fairly long, loose stitch on sheer fabrics so that the fabric does not pucker. Alternatively, slipstitch the hems in place by hand.

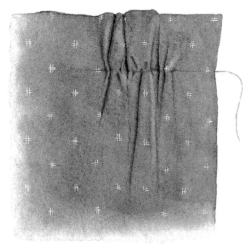

5A

5B

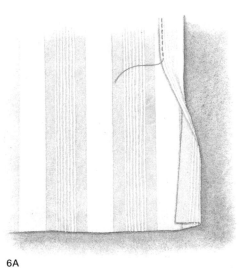

6A

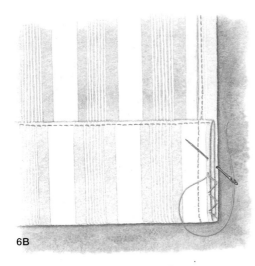

6B

3 If you are using a ready-weighted sheer fabric, move on to step 4, otherwise, press a double 7.5cm (3in) hem along the base of your curtain and stitch in place as for the side hems. To help the curtain hang better, it is advisable to stitch weights inside the base hem before it is caught in place. For lightweight fabrics use lead-weight tape and for heavier fabrics use standard round weights (see page 129 for application). Slipstitch together the open side edges of the base hem (**6B**).

4 Measure the finished curtain length from the base hem and mark with pins. Turn to the appropriate project for instructions on making or attaching the heading tape.

MAKING LINED CURTAINS

There are a number of reasons for lining curtains. It reduces everyday wear and tear, it protects the fabric from the sun's rays, and it helps the curtain to hang and drape better, by adding weight and giving the impression of more fullness. Depending on the type of lining chosen, lined curtains can block out the light rays, cut down on draughts from the windows and give the room some insulation. Lined curtains are best dry-cleaned as the lining and fabric may shrink at different rates.

   The instructions below show how to join fabric widths by machine, but in all other respects the curtains are best made by hand sewing. This is a professional way which gives a much better finish.
1 Cut out the required number of fabric and lining drops, and join widths together, if necessary, with plain straight seams (see page 127).

2 Trim away the joined lining pieces so that they are 10cm (4in) narrower in width than the joined fabric widths. Divide the amount equally between the two outer lining pieces, so that the curtain and lining seams will still match (**7A**).

3 Press a 5cm (2in) hem to the wrong side down each side edge of the main fabric and a 3cm (1¼in) hem to the wrong side down each side edge of the lining. Along the base edge of both fabrics press a double 7.5cm (3in) hem to the wrong side.

4 Mitre the corners of the base edges on both the main fabric and lining (see page 128). Weights can be sewn inside the main curtain base hem (see page 129). Machine stitch the lining base hem in place and slipstitch the base hem in place and the mitred corners together on the main fabric. Stitch the main fabric side hems in place with large herringbone stitches (see page 130) (**7B**).

5 Place the lining on top of the main fabric with wrong sides together, so that the lining side edges are positioned 3cm (1¼in) in from each side edge of the main fabric and 3cm (1¼in) up from the main fabric hem. Check that the seams nearest the leading edge are lying on top of each other. Pin main fabric and lining together along this seam.

6 Working from the pinned seam out to the leading edge, pin the lining to the main fabric at the half-width position. Ensure the lining is flat. Pin and slipstitch the lining side hem in place and also for 5cm (2in) from the corner along the base hem (**7C**).

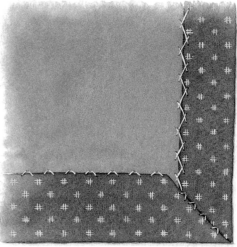

7B

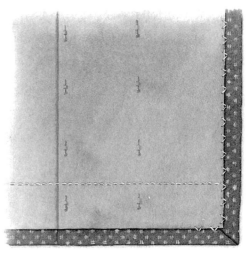

7C

7A

7D

7 Fold the lining back at the pinned seam to reveal the turnings. Using large locking stitches (see page 130), about 10cm (4in) apart, secure the lining and main fabric together (**7D**).

8 Fold the lining back over the main fabric and smooth flat. Pin at the half-width position on the next width of fabric. If you have more than one joined width seam, repeat as before. When the opposite side hem is reached, slipstitch along the side and base of the lining as before. Loosely secure the lining to the base hem at every fabric seam with daisy chain stitches (see page 130).

9 The lining is now secured in place. Measure the finished curtain length from the base hem and mark the position with pins at the top edge of the curtain. Turn to the appropriate project for instructions on making or attaching the heading tape.

8A

8B

MAKING A LINED ROMAN BLIND

Lining a blind gives it more support, protects it from fading and gives insulation. The rod pockets are made only in the lining, so this means that the front of the blind can remain perfectly plain and flat. How deep you choose to make the folds is a matter of taste but the cording rows should always be approximately 30cm (12in) apart, to allow for the blind to fold up neatly.

1 Cut out the main fabric and lining pieces to the correct dimensions and join drops if necessary with plain straight seams (see page 127). On the main fabric press a hem 5cm (2in) deep to the wrong side down both side edges and along the base edge. Mitre the corners (see page 128). Slipstitch the mitred corners together and then stitch all the hems in place with large herringbone stitches (see page 130) (**8A**).

2 On the lining, press a hem 2.5cm (1in) deep to the wrong side down both side edges and tack in place to secure.

3 Working on the wrong side of the lining, measure up from the base edge the pocket spacing that you calculated at the beginning, when estimating your lining quantity, and mark the pocket positions – 5cm (2in) wide – with tailor's chalk (**8B**).

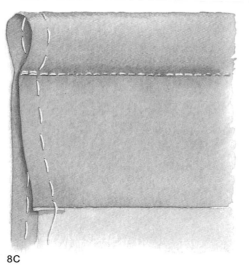

8C

4 With wrong sides facing, fold the lining along the centre of one rod pocket, lining up the chalk lines, and stitch the rod pocket in place 2.5cm (1in) from the fold (**8C**). Repeat for the remaining pockets.

5 Press a 2.5cm (1in) hem to the wrong side along the base edge of the lining and tack in place.

6 Place the lining on top of the main fabric, wrong sides together, so that the side and base edges of the lining are 2.5cm (1in) in and up from the sides and hem of the main fabric. Pin layers together along the hem edge and just below the first rod pocket.

8D

7 Slipstitch the lining base hem to the main fabric hem, then fold back the lining at the pinned rod pocket to reveal the seamline. Using fairly large locking stitches about 10cm (4in) apart (see page 130), secure the lining and the main fabric together along the pocket seamline (**8D**).

8 Fold back the lining over the main fabric and smooth flat. Pin just below the next rod pocket. Repeat as before until the lining is locked to the main fabric along each rod pocket. Slipstitch the lining to the main fabric down both side edges, leaving the ends of the rod pockets open (**8E**).

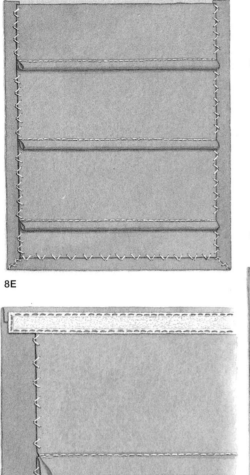

8E

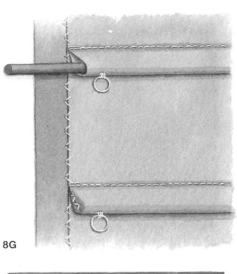

8G

8F

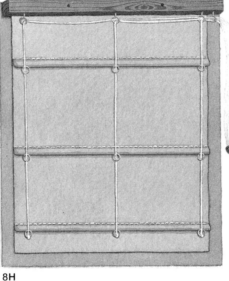

8H

9A

9B

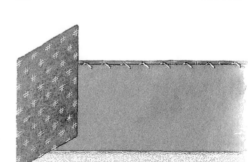

9C

9D

9 Measure the finished length of the blind from the base hem and mark the position of the top edge of the blind with pins. Press the top hem to the wrong side along the pin-line. Trim the hem allowance to 1.5cm (⅝in) and tack in place. Pin the fluffy side of a length of touch-and-close tape to the wrong side of the blind at the top, enclosing the raw edge. Machine stitch in place (**8F**).

10 Hand sew a brass ring to the folded edge of each rod pocket, placing one 5cm (2in) in from each side of the blind, and one centrally between the two. If you want to decorate the blind, do it at this stage (see individual projects). Insert a wooden dowel into each pocket and slipstitch the ends of the pockets closed (**8G**).

11 Fasten the top edge of the blind to the support and, working from the wrong side of the blind, knot a length of fine cord to the bottom rings and thread the cords up through the rest of the rings. Thread the cords through the screw eyes directly above, then pass the cords across so they all pass through the fourth eye. Trim the cords so they are level and attach a toggle to the ends to prevent them slipping back through the screw eyes (**8H**).

12 Screw a cleat to the side of the window frame, so that you can secure the cords firmly in place when the blind is raised. Try to make sure that the cleat is not visible when the blind is raised.

MAKING UP A BOX PELMET

Pelmets are usually cut from plywood or buckram stiffener and covered in fabric. The pelmet is then mounted on a wooden board that sits above the curtain heading (see page 121). The instructions below are for a buckram-stiffened pelmet which is generally simpler to make, economical with fabric and gives a professional finish.

1 Cut out the fabric, lining and interlining pieces to the correct dimensions and join them – main to main and lining to lining. Use lapped seams (see page 128) to join the interlining pieces together.

2 Place the buckram piece centrally on top of the interlining piece so that there is a 2.5cm (1in) allowance around all four edges. Fold the edges of interlining over the buckram, mitre the corners (see page 128) for a neat finish and glue the hem edges down (**9A**). Leave to dry.

3 Machine stitch the fabric and lining together (right sides facing) along one long (top) edge. Press the turnings towards the lining. Pin the fluffy side of a length of touch-and-close tape to the right side of the lining just below the seam and 2.5cm (1in) in from both side edges. Machine stitch in place (**9B**).

4 Place the buckram, interlining side down, on to the wrong side of the main fabric, matching one long edge of the buckram to the main fabric seam. Make sure the fabric is smooth and even across the front, then turn the main fabric 2.5cm (1in) hem allowance over the long base edge of the buckram and tack to the interlining (**9C**). Repeat at the side edges, mitring the corners (see page 128).

5 Fold under the hems on the lining and slipstitch the lining to the fabric through the interlining all around the edges, making sure that the touch-and-close tape remains straight and close to the top edge of the pelmet on the lining side.

6 Measure in from each end of the stiffened pelmet the depth of the pelmet board. Make a fold to the wrong side at these points and press down to make a sharp crease (**9D**). The pelmet is now ready to fit to the pelmet board, by pressing the touch-and-close sections together.

10A

10B

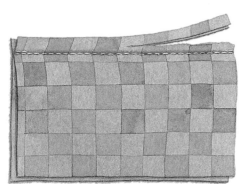

11A

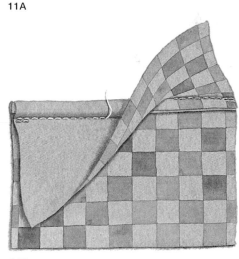

11B

STITCHING BASICS

PLAIN STRAIGHT SEAM

This is the most commonly used seam for joining fabric widths in curtain-making. Use a 2cm (⅜in) seam allowance unless otherwise stated.

1 With right sides together, machine stitch along the seamline, reverse stitching for a few stitches at both ends of the seam to secure the threads (**10A**). For speed and to avoid tacking seams prior to machining, pin seams at right angles to the seamline and then machine slowly over the pins, taking care not to hit one, because it might well break the needle.

2 Using a steam iron, press the seam flat and open (**10B**).

FRENCH SEAM

This is a self-neatening seam, and is used mainly on sheer and lightweight fabrics.

1 With wrong sides facing, pin the two edges together and tack if the fabric is slippery. Machine stitch together 6mm (¼in) from the raw edges. Trim the seam allowances (**11A**).

2 Press the seam open, then refold with right sides together and the original stitchline placed exactly along the folded edge. Press again and pin, then stitch 1cm (⅜in) in from the seamed edge, enclosing the raw edges (**11B**). Press the finished seam to one side.

12A

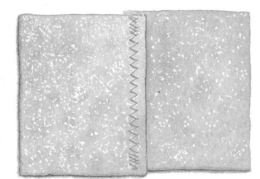

13A

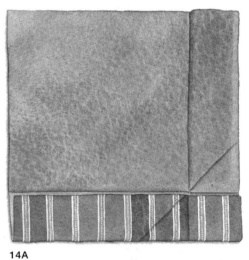

14A

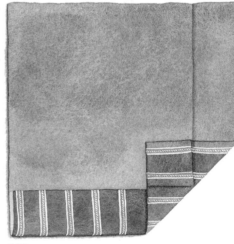

12B

FLAT FELL SEAM

Another self-neatening seam, the flat fell seam, is stronger and flatter than a French seam.

1 With right sides of the fabric together, stitch a plain straight seam. Press the seam allowances open, and then to one side. Trim the seam allowance lying underneath to 6mm (¼in) (**12A**).

2 Fold the edge of the top seam allowance over the trimmed edge, enclosing it. Press this fold flat. Pin at right angles to the seam and stitch it to the main fabric close to the pressed edge (**12B**).

LAPPED SEAM

Interlinings are bulky fabrics, which are best joined with lapped seams to give a completely flat finish.

1 With both pieces of fabric right side up, overlap one of the raw edges directly over the other by approximately 2cm (¾in).

2 Machine stitch the two layers together with a straight or zigzag stitch (**13A**). Trim raw edges.

MITRED CORNERS

Mitres form neat, flat corners, which are particularly useful for bulky fabrics.

1 Press over the required hem allowances down the sides and along the base. (Most projects in this book require a single turned hem for the sides and a double turned hem for the base, but some may vary. The method used for both is the same.)

2 Open out the hems once again. If the base hem is double turned, fold it back up once (**14A**). Then, using the inner finished corner point as a pivot and matching up the press-lines along the side and base (**14B**), fold over the triangular corner.

3 Refold the hems to form the mitre and slipstitch the diagonal edges together (**14C**). If your fabric is very bulky, trim away the fabric at the diagonal corner to a 2cm (¾in) seam turning, before turning the hems back to form the mitre.

14B

14C

15A

15B

WEIGHTS

It is advisable to insert weights into curtain hems, especially when they are floor length.

Lead-weight tape is suitable for lightweight curtains and sheers. It is threaded into the fold of the hem to run the whole width of the curtain and caught in place with daisy chain stitches (see page 130) at intervals inside the hem (**15A**).

For heavier fabrics, standard round weights are better. Some have two holes in the centre so that you can sew them directly to the fabric. They are sewn into the hem at each mitred corner and along the hem – one per fabric

15C

width, or part-width (**15B**). If the weights do not have holes, make small flat bags out of lining (**15C**), and slipstitch these inside the hem to act as weight pockets.

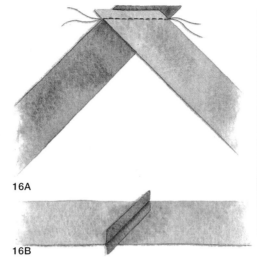

16A

16B

MAKING AND JOINING BINDING STRIPS

When binding straight edges only, the binding strips need not be cut on the bias grain. This makes them easier to cut and it is much more economical with the fabric.

1 Cut straight grain strips of fabric the width required for your binding. Cut enough strips until you have the required length to go around the edge of your project.

2 To join the strips together, you must create a diagonal seam. Either cut strip ends at an angle of 45° or place strips right sides facing at right angles to each other and stitch at 45° (**16A**). Trim the seam turnings and press the seams open (**16B**).

17A

USEFUL STITCHES

The following stitches are worked for a right-handed person; simply reverse the instructions if you are left-handed.

LADDER STITCH

This is a temporary stitch used when joining two pieces of patterned fabric together, where the pattern must be matched across the seam. This is achieved by tacking the fabric pieces together from the right side.

1 Press under the seam allowance along one edge of one piece of fabric and place over the seam allowance of the other so that the pattern matches up exactly. Pin the layers together.

2 Make a knot in a length of thread and bring the needle out under the folded edge. Take the needle out horizontally across the join and down into the flat piece of fabric close to the seamline. Push the needle under the fabric along the seamline, for about 2cm (¾in) and then bring the needle out again and pull the thread through (**17A**).

3 Take a stitch horizontally across the join into the folded edge again, run the needle along the fold for about 2cm (¾in) and then bring the needle out and pull the thread through.

4 Continue in this way until the seam is totally stitched. The two pieces can then be folded right sides together ready for machine stitching.

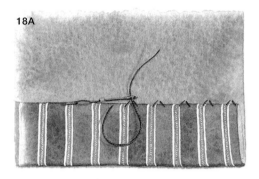

18A

SLIPSTITCH

This stitch is used to hold a folded edge to a flat fabric, and also to hold two folded edges together, as at a mitred corner. It is almost invisible on the right side and is worked from right to left with the needle almost parallel to the stitching line.

1 Bring the needle out of the fold of the fabric and pick up two threads from the fabric directly below.

2 Take the needle back into the folded edge and run the needle inside the fold for approximately 1cm (⅜in). Bring the needle out again and draw the thread through (**18A**). Continue in the same manner, making sure that the stitches are not pulled too tightly, or the fabric will pucker.

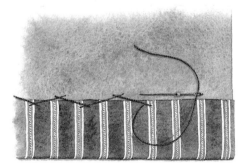

19A

HERRINGBONE STITCH

Used to hold hems firmly in place, this stitch is worked from left to right with the hem fold facing you and the needle pointing to the left.

1 Fasten the working thread and bring the needle up through the hem 3mm (⅛in) in from the edge.

2 Move the needle up and to the right, pick up two threads from the single layer of fabric (**19A**). Pull the needle through. Move the needle down to the right, and take another tiny stitch in the hem. Continue keeping all the stitches the same size.

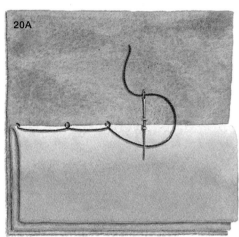

20A

LOCKING STITCH

This stitch is used to hold the lining and interlining loosely to the curtain fabric.

1 Work from left to right with the lining/interlining folded back and nearest to you. Using a thread that matches exactly, secure the thread to the interlining or lining fold. With the needle vertical, make a small stitch by picking up a few threads from the main fabric and the lining/interlining, passing the needle point over the working thread, as shown (**20A**). The two stitches are made in one movement. Draw the needle and thread through, making sure you do not pull the stitch too tight.

2 Make a second stitch 10–15cm (4–6in) to the right, as described above. Continue making stitches spaced 10–15cm (4–6in) apart.

DAISY CHAIN STITCH

This stitch is used to form a small chain to hold the lining to the main fabric at the base edge of a curtain. One end of the chain is attached to the main fabric hem and the opposite end to the lining so that the two layers are linked together.

1 Bring the needle through from the wrong side 1cm (⅜in) below the top of the hem. Make a small stitch on the right side and draw the thread through, leaving a 10cm (4in) loop. Hold the loop open with your thumb and fingers on the left hand, and hold the working thread with the thumb and forefinger of your right hand (**21A**).

2 Reach through the loop with the second finger of your left hand and hook it around the working thread. Draw the working thread back through the loop with your finger (**21B**).

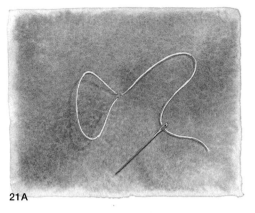

21A

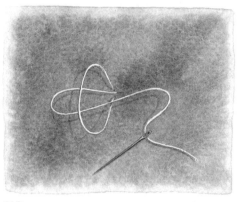

21B

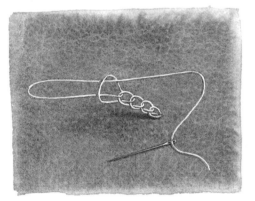

21C

3 As you pull the working thread back, it will begin to form a new loop. Let the first loop slide off your thumb and first finger at the same time, then let it tighten down close to the fabric (**21C**).

4 Hold the new thread as before and continue for 12 stitches. To secure, slip the needle through the last loop, and pull the stitch up tight. Pass the needle into the lining hem opposite and work a couple of stitches. Fasten off the thread.

Assembling the projects

COUNTRY FLANNEL CURTAIN

Ready-made leather tabs are used to hang this unlined curtain from a stylish chrome pole. The curtain is made from men's worsted suiting, bound along the leading edge with mock suede to echo the leather tabs. If you wish, you can make your own tabs for the heading from matching suede or fabric, following the instructions given below, or using one of the kits that are available at good curtain stores and notions counters.

To complete the look, an optional straight tieback, trimmed with mock suede and leather buttons, can be wrapped around the curtain and fastened with touch and-close-tape.

MATERIALS
For the curtain:
- Metal pole without the curtain rings
- Main fabric and mock suede trim (see below for estimating the quantities)
- Matching thread
- Curtain weights (optional)

For the tabs:
- Ready-made leather tabs, or fabric to make your own (see below for estimating the quantities)
- Matching thread
- Leather buttons or clips for attaching the handmade tabs (one for each tab)

For the tiebacks:
- Main fabric, suede trim, and medium-weight interfacing (see below for estimating the quantities)
- Matching thread
- Two 1in. squares of touch-and-close tape
- Two leather buttons

ESTIMATING THE FABRIC
Install your pole and measure your window (see page 120), to find out the finished dimensions of your curtain. For this heading you need fabric 1¼–1½ times your measured curtain width.

For the main curtain fabric: calculate the number of fabric drops required (see page 120). Add 9in. to the curtain length for hem allowances at the top and base, then turn to page 122 to calculate the final fabric quantity.

For the tieback fabric: turn to page 121 to measure for the length. Add 2in. for a wrap and 1¼in. for seam allowances to the length measurement. Then allow for two straight grain pieces, each measuring 5in. deep x the length you have calculated.

For the tieback interfacing: allow for one piece of interfacing – the same size as the tieback.

For the mock suede binding for the curtain: allow for a straight-grain binding strip, 3½in. wide x the length of the curtain, plus hem allowances. For the tieback: allow for two straight-grain binding strips, each 2½in. x the finished length of the tieback, including wrap and seam allowances.

For the tab quantities: to calculate the number of tabs required, subtract 2½in. from the finished width of your curtain and divide the remaining width by 22. Round this figure up to the nearest whole number. If you are making your own tabs, allow for a piece of fabric, or mock suede, 3½ x 11in. for each tab.

MAKING HANDMADE TABS
1 Fold each tab in half lengthwise, right sides together. Stitch the long edges together with a ⅝in. seam allowance, leaving a 1¼in. opening in the center of the seam for turning out.

2 Refold the tab so the seam lies along the center. Lightly press the seam only. Machine stitch across the short ends with a ⅝in. seam allowance (**A**). Clip the corners and turn it right side out. Press the tab flat and slipstitch the opening edges together.

A

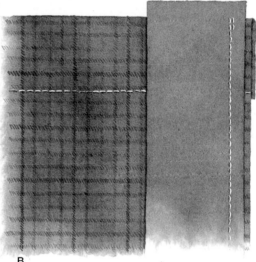

B

MAKING THE CURTAIN
1 Make the curtain following steps 1–3 of Making unlined curtain (page 123), but leave the leading edge unhemmed. Turn over and press a double turned 2in. hem to the wrong side along the top edge and machine stitch in place. On the outer edge of the curtain, slipstitch the open side edges of the top hem together.

2 With right sides together, lay the binding strip on to the curtain's leading edge, with the long raw edges even, and with ⅝in. extending beyond both the top and base of the curtain. Pin, baste and machine stitch in place, taking a ⅝in. seam allowance (**B**).

3 Press the binding toward the leading edge. Turn the curtain over so the wrong side faces up. Fold over a ⅝in. hem on both short ends of the binding strip and press in place. Press over a ⅝in. hem along the remaining long raw edge of the binding strip (**C**). Baste in place.

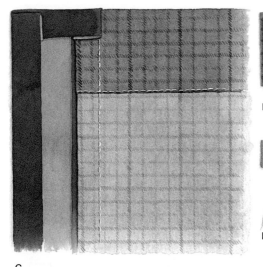

C

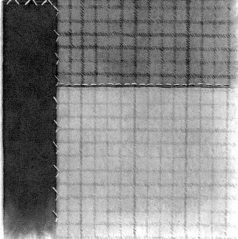

D

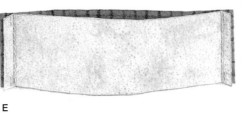

E

F

4 Fold the binding over the leading edge so the folded edge is level with the binding stitchline, enclosing all the raw edges. Pin and slipstitch the loose binding edge to the back of the curtain and slipstitch top and bottom binding edges together (**D**). Remove the basting and pins.

5 Hang the curtain from the pole using the tabs. Position one tab 1¼in. in from each end and those remaining approximately 9in. apart. If you have bought ready-made tabs, use the clips or hooks provided to hang the curtains. If you have made your own tabs, stitch through all layers and use the buttons to hold the tabs in place. If you have used a special kit to make the tabs, use the hardware provided.

MAKING THE TIEBACK

1 Press the interfacing to the wrong side of one tieback piece. With right sides together and raw edges even, machine stitch the two tiebacks together along the two short ends with a ⅝in. seam allowance (**E**).

2 Turn to the right side and press the seams open, then refold the tieback so the stitchlines are placed exactly on the folded edges. Press again, and pin and baste the tieback together along the top and bottom edges.

3 With right sides together, lay one binding strip along the top edge of the tieback with raw edges even and with the short ends extending ⅝in. beyond the seamed ends. Pin, baste and machine stitch the binding in place, with a seam allowance of ⅝in. (**F**). Complete the binding following steps 3 and 4 of the curtain instructions, and then bind the lower edge the same way.

4 Wrap the tieback around the curtain and mark where the ends overlap. Hand-stitch the hook side of a piece of touch-and-close tape to the right side of each tieback at one end. Stitch the fluffy side to the wrong side of the opposite end of the tieback to correspond. Hand-stitch the leather buttons to the right side of the tieback to complete the decoration.

WALL OF SILK

This fully-lined silk curtain is hung from a brass pole that spans the whole width of one wall, not just the window opening. When the curtain is closed it covers the wall completely, creating a sumptuous wall of fabric.

The pencil-pleat heading for this curtain is made by hand, which gives a very professional finish with no telltale double lines of machine stitching. This is perfect for a curtain where the heading is not hidden behind a valance.

MATERIALS

- Brass curtain pole to fit between two walls
- Main fabric and lining (see below for estimating the quantities)
- Matching thread
- Curtain weights (optional)
- 4in. of heading buckram (special heavily stiffened cotton fabric), to fit the ungathered curtain width
- 1¼in-wide webbing to fit finished gathered curtain width
- Strong sewing thread (for hand sewing)
- Pin hooks (with sharp points to push into the back of the heading), or sew-on hooks

ESTIMATING THE FABRIC

Mount the pole between the two side walls as close to the ceiling as possible. Measure for the curtain, taking the width across the whole wall, not just the window (see page 120).

For a handmade pencil-pleat heading, you will need a fabric fullness of 2½–3 times your measured curtain width. Add 11in. to the curtain length for hem allowances at the top and base, then turn to page 122 to calculate the final fabric and lining quantities.

MAKING THE CURTAIN

1 Make the lined curtain following the instructions on page 124. Having marked the finished length with pins at the top edge, turn the top hem to the wrong side along the pinline and press.

A

C

E

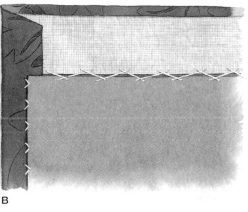

B

D

F

2 Open out the top hem and trim away only the lining along the pinline (do not throw away the lining strip; you will need it later). Herringbone stitch (see page 130) the top edge of the lining to the main fabric (**A**).

3 Place the heading buckram on the top edge of the curtain against the raw edge of the lining, with its short side ends under the side hems of the curtain (**B**). Herringbone stitch the buckram in position along the two long edges, then turn and press the top fabric edge over the buckram and miter the top corners (see page 128) .

4 Fold the stiffened heading down over the lining and slipstitch it in place to secure it along both the side and lower edges.

5 Using strong thread, handsew two parallel lines of running stitches along the heading, matching the stitch lengths exactly. Work one row ⅜in from the top edge and the second row 3¼in. below. Leave the ends of the threads loose, and use a new piece of thread for each fabric width in your curtains (**C**). Pull up the threads to gather the top to the finished curtain width. Knot the thread ends.

6 Trim the leftover lining strip to the same length as the webbing: this should be the finished gathered curtain width, plus ⅜in. Stitch the strip of lining to the back of the webbing, overlapping the long edges by approximately ⅝in. and letting the lining ends extend ⅜in. at each end (**D**).

7 Handstitch the webbing to the back of the heading about ⅝in. below the top of the curtain; the lining strip should hang below the webbing. Make sure it is stitched firmly in place around all edges, catching into the heading buckram with each stitch.

8 If you are using pin hooks, move on to step 9. For sew-on curtain hooks, space them evenly along the webbing. Stitch the hooks firmly in place using strong thread, making sure your stitches pass through all layers of fabric (**E**).

9 Press over the short ends of the lining strip level with the webbing ends. Fold the long loose edge of the lining strip up over the webbing, leaving the hooks showing. Tuck under the raw edge and slipstitch the lining strip along the top and sides (**F**). If using pin hooks, insert them at even intervals into the back of the covered webbing strip.

A

B

C

SUITING & SATIN

A camel-colored suiting fabric has been used in this room to make a pair of unlined gathered curtains and three matching Roman shades. Both the curtains and shades are edged with a complementary colored satin binding, and their headings are hidden behind plaster coving at the ceiling. Three lined Roman shades have been used to span a very wide window; they are corded so they pull up and down together, from one side.

MATERIALS

For the unlined curtains:
- Main fabric and contrasting binding fabric (see below for estimating quantities)
- Matching thread
- 1¼in-wide gathered heading tape, to fit the width of the ungathered curtain
- Cord holder

For each lined Roman shade:
- Fabric, lining, and contrasting binding fabric (see below for estimating quantities)
- Matching thread
- Touch-and-close tape to fit the width of the finished shade (see page 126)
- Brass rings (3 per casing)
- Wooden dowels (1 per casing), ⅜in. in diameter, the finished width of the shade minus 2in.

For all Roman shades collectively:
- 2 x 1in. wooden support, to fit the total width of the window
- Ten large screw eyes
- Thin cord
- One toggle end and cleat

ESTIMATING THE FABRIC

For the curtains, mount the track on the wall or ceiling behind the coving and measure your window (see page 120) to establish the finished width and length of your curtain. For a gathered heading you will need a fabric fullness of 1½ times your measured curtain width. Add 3¼in. to the length for a top hem allowance, then turn to page 122 to work out your final fabric requirement.

For the Roman shades: prepare the wooden support for faced-fmounted shades to fit the total width of the window (see page 121), but do not screw the eyes into the wood just yet. Secure the support in place. Measure the length of the support and divide it into three equal sections to calculate the finished width of each shade; turn to page 121 to calculate the finished length for a face-mounted shade. Add 2in. to the length measurement of the main fabric only, for a hem allowance at the top. For the lining, remember not to add any hem allowances, but turn to page 122 to calculate the quantity.

For the curtain binding: allow for two straight-grain strips, 6in. wide. Each should be the length of the finished curtain, plus the width of the ungathered curtain, plus another 4in.

For the binding for each shade: allow one strip 8in. wide, multiplied by twice the finished length and once the finished width. Then add 6in. to the total length. You will have to join lengths of binding together to make up the correct lengths (see page 129).

MAKING THE CURTAINS

1 Cut out the required number of fabric drops and join any widths together with flat-fell seams (see page 128). Press a double-turned ⅝in hem to the wrong side along the outer side edges. Machine or slipstitch in place (see page 130).

2 Measure the finished length of the curtain from the raw base edge and mark with a line of pins. Measure 1¼in. above the pinline and fold the top hem over to the wrong side at this point. Press and then remove the pins.

3 Starting at the raw leading edge, position the heading tape on the wrong side of the curtain, 1¼in. below the pressed top edge (the raw edges should now be covered). Secure the cords with a knot on the wrong side of the tape and pin the tape in place. Cut off the tape at the opposite end, leaving ⅝in. for folding under, and leave the cord ends free.

4 Starting at the lower edge of the tape heading on the leading edge, machine stitch up the short edge of the tape, along the top and down the short edge at the opposite end (**A**). Then again starting at the leading edge, machine stitch along the lower edge of the tape, making sure the fabric below is kept smooth and flat; otherwise, the curtain may pucker when the tape is pulled up.

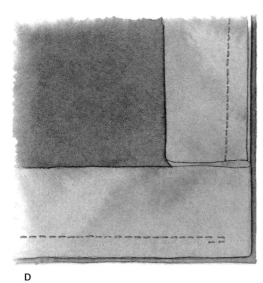

D

E

F

5 With wrong sides together, fold the binding strip in half lengthwise, keeping raw edges even, and press. Starting at the top of the curtain, place the doubled binding to the right side of the curtain leading edge, letting the binding strip extend ⅜in. above the curtain top and keeping the raw edges level. Machine stitch the binding in place with a 1in. seam allowance, stopping 1in. from the base corner, and working a few reverse stitches (**B**).

6 Fold the loose end of the binding up and to the right, making a 45° angle (**C**). Keeping the diagonal fold in place, fold the binding back down, aligning the raw edges with the base edge of the curtain. Starting at the point where the last stitch ended, stitch the binding in place along the bottom edge to the outer curtain edge (**D**).

7 To miter the binding at the leading edge base corner, fold the curtain so the leading edge and base bindings lie on top of each other. Pull the curtain fabric out of the way. Starting at the end of the binding stitching line, sew diagonally across the binding up to the center of the folded edge. Clip diagonally into the binding seam allowances, close to the stitching line (**E**).

8 Press over the short ends of the binding level with the top and outer edges of the curtain, then fold the binding on to the back of the curtain. On the wrong side, fold a mitre at the base corner. Slipstitch the pressed edge of the binding in place, just covering the machine stitches, and enclosing the raw edge of the heading tape on the leading edge (**F**). Stitch together the open ends of the binding at the top and outer edges using slipstitch.

9 Pull up the cords in the heading tape evenly to the required finished curtain width, and knot together the cord ends. Wind the loose ends around the cord tidy and secure in place. Never cut off the excess cords, because this means that the curtains can not be pulled out flat again for cleaning. Arrange the gathers evenly across the curtain and hang the curtains from the track.

MAKING THE ROMAN BLINDS

1 Cut out the main fabric, lining and binding pieces to the correct dimensions and join any pieces with plain, straight seams (see page 127). Prepare and attach the binding to the side and base edges of the blind, as you did with the unlined curtain (steps 5 - 7 above).

2 Trim the short ends of the binding level with the top edges of the blind, then fold the binding on to the back of the blind around the three sides. On the wrong side, fold a mitre at each of the base corners, pin the binding in place and then herringbone stitch (see page 130) the pressed edge of the binding to the main blind fabric.

3 Continue making the blind following the lined Roman blind instructions (see page 125, step 2 to step 10). Using a bradawl, mark the positions of the screw eyes on the timber support (lining them up with the rows of cording rings on each blind), and screw them in place. Screw an extra eye 2.5cm (1in) in from one end of the support, at the cord operating end. Hang the three blinds following steps 11 and 12 of the lined Roman blind instructions (see page 126), passing each cord along through the top screw eyes so that they all pass through the final eye at the operating end.

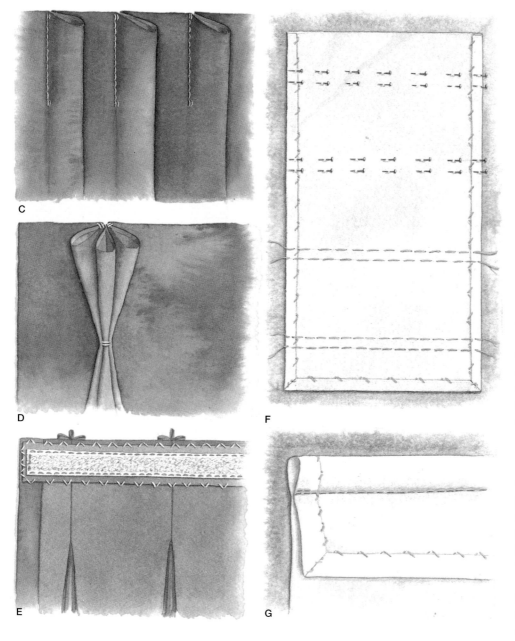

C

D

E

F

G

7 Turn each large pleat into three smaller pleats. Working with one pleat at a time, open out the top edge with your fingers and push in each side of the pleat to the stitching line to form three equally sized pleats. Make a crease down the buckram to hold the new pleats in place. Using strong thread, hand-stitch the group of three pleats together at the base of the heading buckram at the outer creased edges. Hand-stitch the tops in place separately at the inner fold of each pleat, forming a sort of fan (**D**). Repeat until all the triple pleats are formed.

8 Press a 1cm (⅜in) hem to the wrong side along the lining strip and place the fluffy side of the touch-and-close tape on to the right side of the strip. Machine stitch in place around all the edges.

9 Place the lining strip on to the wrong side of the curtain heading just below the top edge, with the touch-and-close tape uppermost. Hand-stitch the strip to the back of the heading, making sure it is firmly stitched in place around all the edges and caught into the heading buckram with each stitch (**E**). Hang the curtain from the shaped pelmet board by pressing the touch-and-close tape sections together.

MAKING THE SHEER ROMAN BLIND

1 Cut out the required number of fabric drops and join widths together, if necessary, with flat fell seams (see page 128). Turn and press a double 3cm (1¼in) hem along the side edges and along the lower edge. Mitre the lower corners (see page 128), and slipstitch corners and hems in place.

2 Working on the wrong side of the blind, measure up from the base hem the pocket spacing you calculated when you were estimating your fabric requirements. Mark the 5cm (2in) wide rod pockets with pins across the blind. Work large tacking stitches along each pin-line and remove the pins (**F**).

3 With right sides facing, fold the fabric along the centre of one rod pocket, lining up the tacking lines, and stitch the rod pocket in place following the tacking line, 2.5cm (1in) from the fold (**G**). Repeat for the remaining rod pockets, and remove all tacking stitches. Complete the blind following steps 9 to 12 of the lined Roman blind instructions (see page 126).

5 Subtract the finished curtain width from the width of the flat made-up curtain (minus 16cm [6in]) to allow for an 8cm (3in) return (R) at each end of the curtain heading, then divide the remaining amount by the number of spaces. Working on the wrong side of the curtain and starting at the leading edge, mark the pleat positions with pins along the top edge of the curtain heading (**B**).

6 With lining sides facing, fold the curtain at the heading to bring the first two pins together to form one large pleat. Making sure that the top edges are level, crease the buckram firmly along the fold. Machine stitch the pleat in place from the pin position at the top edge down for 13cm (5in); keep the stitching parallel to the fold, and reverse stitch very neatly at each end of the stitch-line to secure. Form the remaining pleats along the heading in the same way (**C**).

BRIGHT STRIPES

The banners for this project are formed from separate bands of crisp unlined linen fabric in bold colours, which are attached to the curtain heading tape using touch-and-close tape. The fully-lined curtains are made with a special fluffy pencil-pleat heading tape, which allows the hook side of the touch-and-close tape to stick to it. The track and headings are then concealed by a fabric-covered box pelmet, which can be made to match either the banner or the curtain fabric.

MATERIALS

For the lined curtains:
- Main fabric and lining
  (see below for estimating the quantities)
- Matching thread
- Curtain weights (optional)
- Fluffy pencil-pleat heading tape (see above)
  to fit the width of the ungathered curtain
- Cord tidy

For the banners:
- Crisp firm fabrics
  (see below for estimating the quantities)
- Matching thread
- 45cm (18in) of touch-and-close tape
  for each banner

For the box pelmet:
- Curtain track
- A 12–18cm (5–7in) deep pelmet board,
  fitted in place
- Fabric, lining, and bump or domette interlining
  (see below for estimating quantities)
- Matching thread
- Buckram or other stiffener, the same size
  as the finished pelmet, including returns
  (see page 120 for measuring up)
- Fabric glue
- Touch-and-close tape to fit the length
  of the finished pelmet, including returns

ESTIMATING THE FABRIC

For the curtains, fix your track in place to the underside of the pelmet board and measure your window (see page 120) to find out the finished width and length of your curtain. When measuring the length, take into consideration that, for this style, the curtains will need to hang from the centre row of pockets on the heading tape, to allow for the banner attachment. For a pencil-pleat heading, you will need a fabric fullness of 2½–3 times your measured curtain width. Add 20cm (8in) to the curtain length for hem allowances at the top and base, then turn to page 122 to work out your final fabric and lining quantities.

For each banner, allow for a length equal to the curtain length plus 19cm (7½in) for hem allowances at the top and base. Allow for a width of 50cm (20in) including hem allowances.

Turn to page 122 to work out how much fabric, lining and interlining you will need for the pelmet.

MAKING THE CURTAINS

1 Make the lined curtains following the instructions on page 124. Having marked the finished length with pins, turn over and press the top hem to the wrong side along the pin-line (**A**). This hem allowance will be concealed by the heading tape, so if there is too much just trim some away.

2 Starting at the leading edge, position the heading tape on the wrong side of the curtain, close to the top edge. Fold under about 1.5cm (⅝in) of tape at one end and secure the cords with a knot on the wrong side of the tape. Pin the tape in place. Cut off the heading tape at the opposite end, leaving 1.5cm (⅝in) for folding under, and leave the cord ends free.

3 Starting at the lower edge of the tape on the leading edge, machine stitch up the short edge of the tape, along the top and down the opposite short edge (**B**). Again starting at the leading edge, machine stitch along the lower edge of the tape, ensuring that the fabric below is kept smooth and flat, otherwise the curtain may pucker when the heading tape is pulled up.

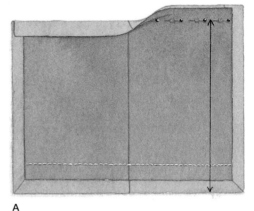

A

B

4 Pull the cords evenly to gather the curtain to the finished width required and knot the cord ends together. Wind the loose ends around the cord tidy and secure in place. Do not cut off the excess cords, as this would mean that the curtains could never be pulled out flat for cleaning. Arrange the pleats evenly and hang the curtains from the track.

MAKING A BANNER

1 Press a double 1.5cm (⅝in) hem along both side edges and machine stitch, or slipstitch, in place.

2 Press a double 7.5cm (3in) hem to the wrong side along the base of the banner and machine stitch, or slipstitch, in place. Slipstitch closed the open side edges of the base hem.

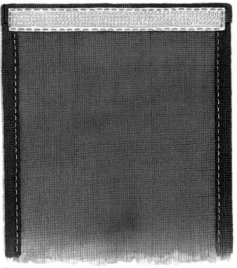

C

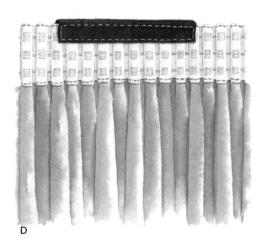

D

3 Pin a single 1.5cm (⅝in) hem to the wrong side along the top edge of the banner. Tack in place. Pin the hook side of the touch-and-close tape to the wrong side of the banner at the top, enclosing the raw edge. Machine stitch the tape in place (**C**).

4 Draw the curtains closed and position the banner 45cm (18in) in from the leading edge, with the hem edges level. Wrap the hook tape at the top of the banner over the curtain heading and press to the heading tape to fix in place (**D**).

MAKING THE BOX PELMET

Make up the pelmet following the instructions for a box pelmet on page 127.

ALPACA THROW

An alpaca furnishing fabric has been used to make this unlined dress curtain, with its separate throw heading. The curtain is hung from a wooden pole, while the throw is draped over it, arranged in pleats to fall halfway down the curtain. The throw is bound on all sides with mock suede, and the ends of the wooden pole are decorated with sheaves covered in fabric and strips of contrasting leather.

MATERIALS

For the unlined curtain:
- Wooden pole
- Main fabric (see below for estimating the quantities)
- Matching thread
- 3cm (1¼in) wide gathered heading tape, to fit the width of the ungathered curtain
- Cord tidy

For the throw:
- 5m (5½yd) of 120–135cm (48–54in) wide fabric
- Matching thread
- Contrast mock suede binding fabric (see below for estimating the quantities)

For the pole ends:
- Two 25cm (10in) squares of fabric
- Two 18cm (7in) lengths of chrome tubing, the diameter to fit over the wooden curtain pole with some clearance
- Fabric glue
- Masking tape
- Leather thongs in two colours

ESTIMATING THE FABRIC

For the curtain, fix the pole to the wall and measure your window (see page 120) to find out the finished width and length of your curtain. For a gathered heading, you will need a fabric fullness of 1½ times your measured curtain width. Add 28cm (11in) to the curtain length for hem allowances at the top and base, then turn to page 122 to work out how much fabric you will need.

For the throw binding, allow for a straight-grain strip 9cm (3½in) wide, and 10m (10¾yd) long. Join the lengths of binding together to obtain the correct length (see page 129).

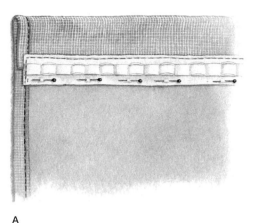

A

MAKING THE CURTAIN

1 Make the curtain following the instructions for an unlined curtain on page 123. Having marked the finished length with pins, measure 3cm (1¼in) above the pin-line and press the top hem over to the wrong side at this point. Remove the pins.

2 From the leading edge, position the heading tape on the wrong side of the curtain, 3cm (1¼in) below the pressed top edge (trim excess from the raw edges). Fold under about 1.5cm (⅝in) of the tape at one end and secure the cords on the wrong side of the tape. Pin the tape in place. Leaving 1.5cm (⅝in) for folding under, and leaving the cord ends free, cut off the tape at the opposite end.

3 Starting at the lower edge of the tape on the leading edge, machine stitch up the short edge, along the top and down the opposite short edge (**A**). Again starting at the leading edge, machine stitch along the lower edge of the tape, ensuring that the fabric below is kept smooth, otherwise the curtain may pucker when the tape is pulled up.

4 Pull up the cords evenly to the finished curtain width required and knot the cord ends together. Wind the loose ends around the cord tidy and secure in place. Do not cut off the excess cords, as this would mean that the curtain could never be pulled out flat for cleaning. Arrange the gathers evenly and hang the curtain from the pole.

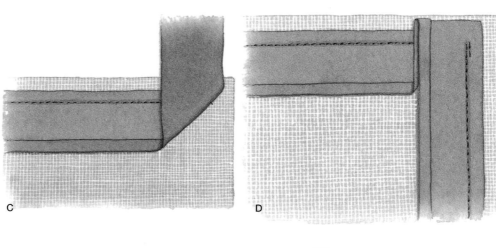

B

C

D

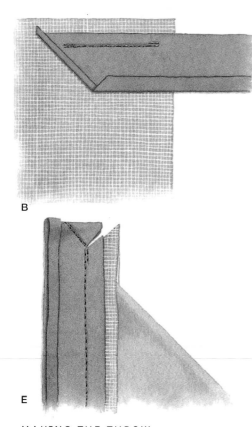

E

F

MAKING THE THROW

1 Cut the fabric into two pieces of equal length and trim off the selvedges. Join the two pieces together along one long edge with a flat fell seam (see page 128), to make one large square.

2 Cut the starting end of the binding strip at a 45° angle, fold a 6mm (¼in) turning to the wrong side along the cut end and press in place. Fold one long edge of the binding strip 1.5cm (⅝in) to the wrong side and press in place.

3 Starting at the centre of one of the long edges, place the binding on to the throw with right sides together, and the long raw edge of the binding 1.5cm (⅝in) in from the edge of the throw. Starting 1cm (⅜in) in from the diagonal pressed edge, machine stitch the binding in place, reverse stitching to secure and working with a 1.5cm (⅝in) seam allowance 3cm (1¼in) in from the throw edges. Stop 3cm (1¼in) in from the corner and work a few reverse stitches (**B**).

4 Fold the loose working end of the binding up, making a 45° angle (**C**). Keeping the diagonal fold in place, fold the binding back down, aligning the raw edge parallel to the next side of the throw, but 1.5cm (⅝in) in from the edge. Starting at the point where the last stitch ended, stitch the binding in place along the next side of the throw (**D**).

5 Continue in the same way, until the binding is stitched in place around all four edges of the throw. Tuck the finishing end of the binding inside the diagonal starting section.

6 To mitre the binding at the corners, fold the throw at each corner so that the bindings lie on top of each other. Pull the throw fabric out of the way. Starting at the end of the binding stitch-line, sew diagonally across the binding up to the centre of the folded edge. Snip diagonally into the binding seam turnings, close to the stitch-line (**E**).

7 Turn the pressed edge of the binding on to the back of the throw. Machine stitch or slipstitch the folded edge of the binding in place just covering the binding machine stitches, and folding a mitre at each corner to neaten.

8 Drape the throw over the pole above the curtain and let it hang down equally at the back and front of the curtain. Neatly arrange the throw into loose pleats for a decorative effect.

MAKING THE POLE ENDS

1 For each pole end, press a 2.5cm (1in) hem to the wrong side along one side of a fabric square. Fold two small pleats in the square 1cm (⅜in) apart, parallel to the pressed edge (**F**) and preferably matching each other. Carefully press the pleats in place.

2 Wrap the fabric around a chrome tube with the pleated end approximately 1cm (⅜in) in from one end of the tube. Tuck the raw ends into the opposite end of the tube and glue the fabric in place (use masking tape to hold the fabric in place until the glue is dry).

3 Wrap strips of leather thong around each end of the fabric-covered tube and glue the strips in place (use masking tape to hold them in place until the glue is dry). Slide a decorated end on to each end of the pole, with the pleats to the outer edges.

LONG WHITE SHEER

It is hard to use a curtain track with a shaped window, so this pretty sheer curtain is simply fastened to the top of the window using touch-and-close tape. It can be left hanging loose or pulled back from the window with a very narrow tieback made from the same fabric as the curtain.

MATERIALS

- Touch-and-close tape to fit curved window top
- Sheer fabric (see below for estimating the quantity)
- Matching thread
- Brown paper, old wallpaper or lining paper for a template
- Tieback hook (optional)

ESTIMATING THE FABRIC

Fasten the hook side of the touch-and-close tape to the top shaped edge of the window with staples. Measure your window to find the finished width and length of your curtain (see page 120); for the finished length, measure the window from the tallest point at the top edge of the touch-and-close tape. You will need a fabric fullness of 2 times your measured curtain width for the tucked heading. Add 20cm (8in) to the curtain length for a hem allowance at the top and base, then turn to page 122 to work out what fabric you will need.

MAKING THE CURTAIN

1 Make the curtain following the instructions for an unlined curtain on page 123. Using brown paper, wallpaper or newspaper, trace around the top shaped edge of the window, where the tape is attached, and cut it out to form a template.

2 Measure the width of the flat made-up curtain and subtract the finished width of the window to calculate the amount of fabric left for the pleats. The pleats should be spaced approximately 10cm (4in) apart, so to find out how many pleats you need, divide the window width by 10cm (4in) – to give you the number of spaces – and subtract one. For example, nine spaces will mean eight pleats. Divide the amount of fabric available for pleats by the number of pleats to find the size of each pleat.

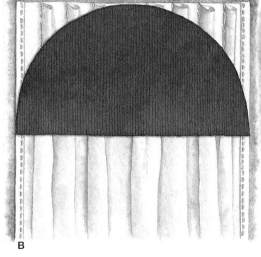

A

B

C

D

3 Working on the wrong side of the curtain, mark the pleat positions with pins along the top edge of the curtain and again 25cm (10in) down from the top edge. With right sides together, fold the curtain at the top, bringing the first two sets of pins together to form a vertical pleat. Making sure that the top edges are level, tack the pleat in place and fold to one side (**A**). Form the remaining pleats in the same way.

4 Lay the template on the curtain with its top curved edge placed up to the straight curtain top, and its straight side edges level with the curtain sides. Using tailor's chalk, draw around the template's curved edge (**B**). Re-tack the pleats in place just below the chalk line and then cut along the line to shape the top.

5 Press a 1cm (⅜in) hem to the wrong side along the curved edge and tack the fluffy side of the touch-and-close tape to this edge, enclosing the raw edge. Machine stitch in place around all edges of the tape (**C**). Remove the tacking stitches and hang the curtain by pressing the touch-and-close tape sections together.

MAKING THE TIEBACK

Cut a straight-grain strip of fabric 4cm (1½in) wide and 75cm (30in) long from the curtain waste fabric. With right sides together, fold the strip in half lengthways, keeping raw edges level. Stitch the strip together along one short end and the long side (**D**). Snip the corners and turn the strip through to the right side, using a knitting needle or similar object. Tuck the raw end into the tube and slipstitch (see page 130) the edges together. Tie the strip around the curtain and loop it over a tieback hook at the side of the window.

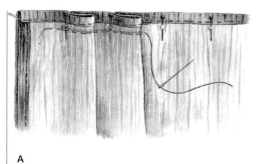

A

B

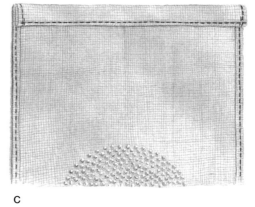

C

SILVER BEADED SHEERS

This project features two unlined dress curtains, hung one in front of the other. The back curtain is a sheer panel beautifully decorated with beads and threaded on to a net rod at the top. The full-length front curtain is made from a metallic crinkle fabric, clipped on to a chrome pole at the top; it can be swept back with a silver cord tieback to reveal the beaded panel beneath.

MATERIALS

For the long curtain:

- Chrome pole and clip-on curtain rings
- Metallic crinkle fabric (see below for estimating the quantity)
- Matching thread
- 2cm (¾in) wide cotton tape or webbing, the width of the finished curtain
- 75cm (30in) of thick silver cord for tieback
- Tieback hook

For the sheer panel:

- Net curtain rod
- Sheer beaded fabric panel (see below for estimating the quantity)
- Matching thread

ESTIMATING THE FABRIC

Fasten the curtain pole just above the window, and the net rod to the top of the window frame. To work out the width and length of your curtains, turn to page 120; measure down to the floor for the long front curtain and to the window-sill for the sheer panel. For the tucked heading on the long curtain, you will need a fabric fullness of 2 times your measured curtain width. Add 20cm (8in) to the curtain length for hem allowances at the top and base. Turn to page 122 to calculate how much fabric you will need to buy.

For the sheer beaded panel, add 5cm (2in) to the finished width measurement, and 20cm (8in) to the length for hems at the top and base. Remember to allow for any decoration to be placed centrally in the window.

MAKING THE LONG CURTAIN

1 Make the curtain following the instructions for making an unlined curtain on page 123. After marking the finished length with pins, press the top hem over to the wrong side along the pin-line. This hem allowance will be concealed by cotton tape, so if there is too much, trim some away. Tack the hem.

2 Measure the width of the flat made-up curtain and subtract the finished width of the curtain; this will give you the amount of fabric left for the pleats. To find out how many pleats you need, and allowing for spacing them approximately 10cm (4in) apart, divide the window width by 10cm (4in). This gives you the number of spaces, and you will need one less pleat. Divide the amount of fabric for pleats by the number of pleats to find the size of each pleat.

3 Working on the wrong side of the curtain, mark the pleat positions with pins along the top edge of the curtain. With right sides together, fold the curtain at the top bringing the first two pins together to form a pleat. Making sure that the top edges are level, fold the pleat to one side and tack it in place (**A**). Form the remaining pleats in the same way.

4 Fold under about 1.5cm (⅝in) of the cotton tape at one end and pin to the top edge of the curtain, enclosing the raw edge. Leaving a further 1.5cm (⅝in) for folding under, cut off the tape at the opposite end. Machine stitch round all the edges to secure the tape (**B**). Remove the tacking stitches and hang the curtain on the pole, clipping each curtain ring to the top of a pleat. Tie the cord around the curtain and loop it over a tieback hook at the side of the window.

MAKING THE SHEER PANEL

1 Make the panel following the instructions for an unlined curtain on page 123. Having marked the finished length with pins, check that the top hem allowance is 5cm (2in); if there is too much spare fabric, just trim some away.

2 To form the top channel for the net rod, press the top raw edge 2cm (¾in) to the wrong side, and then press over another 3cm (1¼in). Machine stitch in place close to the first pressed edge (**C**). Thread the sheer panel on to the net rod and hang it behind the curtain.

HOOKED PANEL BLIND

This is perhaps the easiest form of face-fixed blind as it has no mechanism or cording system to raise it and lower. Made from a beautiful unlined metallic fabric, the blind is simply hung on two hooks at the top corners.

MATERIALS
- Fabric (see below for estimating the quantity)
- Two 10cm (4in) squares of medium-weight iron-on interfacing
- Matching thread
- Two large metal eyelets
- Two decorative hooks

A

B

ESTIMATING THE FABRIC

First measure your window; see page 120 to find out the finished length and width for a face-fixed blind. You will need to add 40cm (16in) to the length measurement for the top and base hems and add on 30cm (12in) to the width measurement for the side hems.

If your fabric is not wide enough for your blind, you will have to allow for a piece of fabric to be stitched down each side. These panels should be of an equal width. It is best to turn any joins into a design feature of the blind; this will use more fabric, but look far superior. To do this, allow for double the width of fabric you require for each side of the blind. Remember to allow for the top and base hem allowances as well as a 2cm (¾in) seam allowance down each side of the extra pieces and down each side of the main fabric piece.

MAKING THE BLIND

1 Cut out the blind and join widths if necessary (see step 3).

2 On a blind made from a single piece of fabric, position the interfacing squares 3cm (1¼in) in and down from the raw edges on the wrong side of the blind at the top two corners and press to fuse to fabric. Turn and press a 2.5cm (1in) hem to the wrong side down both side edges of the blind. Tack the hems, then press over another 13cm (5¼in) to the wrong side and pin. Slipstitch the hems in place, enclosing the raw edges (**A**). Continue making up from step 5.

3 To attach pieces to the sides if your fabric is not wide enough, machine stitch, with right sides together, one long edge of each side piece to the side edges of the blind, taking a 2cm (¾in) seam. Press the seams towards the side pieces. Press the interfacing squares to the wrong side of each side piece at the two top corners, 3cm (1¼in) in and down from the raw edges (**B**), as before.

4 Press to the wrong side a 2cm (¾in) hem down each remaining long edge of the side pieces and tack. Fold one side piece over on to the wrong side of the blind, so that the line of the tacked hem lies along the machine stitchline. Pin and slipstitch the hem edge along the stitchline (**C**). Press the side extension. Repeat with the remaining piece.

C

D

5 Press a 13cm (5¼in) deep hem to the wrong side along the top edge of the blind, then press over another 13cm (5¼in) to form a doubled hem. Pin and then slipstitch the hem in place. Along the base of the blind make a double 7.5cm (3in) hem. Slipstitch together the open ends of the top and base hems to close the sides.

6 Mark the positions for the eyelets on the top hem at the outer corners, making sure that they sit on the interfacing squares (which will reinforce the fabric). Insert the eyelets using a special eyelet tool, or ask a specialist company to insert them for you (**D**). Screw the hooks to the wall in line with the eyelets and hang the blind from them. To open the blind, simply unhook one side of the blind and allow it to drape from one hook.

ROLL-UP & ROLL-DOWN BLINDS

Although in principle these two blinds both roll up and down, and look similar, they are in fact made and operated in very different ways. The first is a reverse roller blind operated with cords, rather like a Roman blind. The other is a spring-loaded roller blind fitted to the base of the window; they are usually fitted the other way up. This blind is operated by pulling it upwards and clipping the top batten over hooks at the sides of the window.

MATERIALS

For the reverse roller blind:

- 5 x 2.5cm (2 x 1in) timber support to fit the width of the window recess
- Five large screw eyes
- Fabric (see below for estimating the quantity)
- Matching thread
- Touch-and-close tape to fit the width of the finished blind
- Fine cord
- Toggle end and cleat

For the base roller blind:

- Roller blind kit to fit the width of the window recess
- Pre-stiffened fabric, or a smooth, firm, closely woven fabric (see below for estimating the quantity)
- Fabric stiffener (if fabric is not pre-stiffened)
- Matching thread
- Masking tape
- Four tieback hooks
- Touch-and-close tape (optional)

ESTIMATING THE FABRIC

For the reverse roller blind, prepare the timber support for a recess-fixed blind (see page 121), attaching the hook side of the touch-and-close tape to the top and leaving out the screw eyes for the present. Fix the support to the frame, halfway up the window, screwing it in position from front to back. Measure your window (see page 120) to find the finished dimensions of the blind. Add 20cm (8in) to the length measurement for hem and rolling allowances, and 5cm (2in) to the width, for the side hems. If you need more than one fabric width for your blind, allow for a full fabric width to be placed centrally, with any part-widths down each side.

For the base roller blind, see page 121 for positioning the brackets into the window recess just above the sill, and measuring the length of the roller. Remember that you are fitting the blind upside down, so you may need to reverse the brackets to mirror the top of the window; check the fitting instructions with the kit. This blind needs to be made from one piece of fabric, without joins. For the fabric width, measure the roller from the end of the square pin to the end of the round pin and subtract 3cm (1¼in) for pre-stiffened fabric (this fabric will not fray and therefore needs no side hems); take away 1cm (⅜in) for fabric that needs stiffening (allowing for side hems). For the length, measure from the roller to halfway up the window, and add 30cm (12in).

MAKING THE REVERSE ROLLER BLIND

1 Fix two of the screw eyes to the underside of the timber support, placing them about 20cm (8in) in from each end; this is where the operating cords will attach. With a bradawl, prepare the holes for the screw eyes in the front of the support, positioning two in line with the eyes below and the final one very close to the operating side (**A**).

2 Cut out the required number of fabric drops and join the widths together with flat fell seams (see page 128). Press a double 1.5cm (⅝in) hem along the side edges and machine stitch in place. Press a double 2cm (¾in) hem to the wrong side along the lower edge and stitch in place, close to the first fold.

3 Press over a 1.5cm (⅝in) hem to the wrong side along the top edge and tack in place. Pin the fluffy side of the touch-and-close tape to the wrong side of the blind at the top, enclosing this raw edge. Machine stitch round all the edges of the tape to fix in place.

4 Fasten the top edge of the blind to the support by pressing the touch-and-close tape sections together. Knot a length of fine cord to the screw eyes underneath the timber support. Pierce the blind fabric with the bradawl at the three front screw eye positions. Using the bradawl, wiggle the weave apart on the fabric to form holes large enough for the eyes. Carefully insert the eyes, trying not to twist the fabric as you screw them in (**B**).

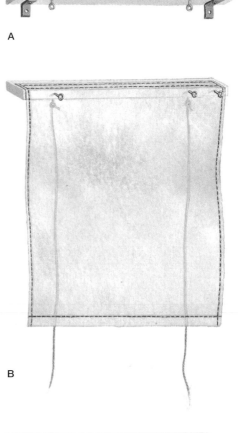

A

B

C

5 Get someone to help you roll up the blind from the bottom, facing towards you, and hold it parallel to the sill, while you bring the cords round to the front. Thread them through the corresponding eyes on the front of the support and pass them both across the top of the blind to thread through the eye at the side (**C**).

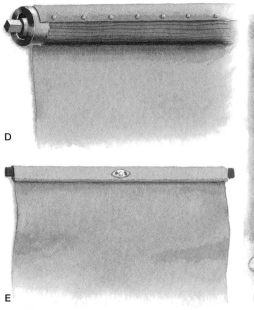

D

E

F

6 Check that the blind rolls up parallel, by slowly pulling on the cords, then let it down (the bottom of the blind should always remain partially rolled, to help with the momentum). Trim the cords level and attach a toggle to the ends. Then screw the cleat to the side of the frame, so that the cords can be secured in place when the blind is raised.

MAKING THE BASE ROLLER BLIND

1 For pre-stiffened fabric, start at step 2. If your fabric needs stiffening, do this before cutting to size in case it shrinks. Press out any fabric creases and hang the fabric in a well-ventilated area. Spray both sides well with fabric stiffener, but do not over-wet the fabric. Leave to hang until dry.

2 Cut out the fabric using a set square to ensure that the right-angled corners are perfect. If not, the blind will not roll properly. (Continue from step 4 for the pre-stiffened fabric.)

3 Press 1cm (⅜in) turnings to the wrong side along both side edges and machine in place with a zigzag stitch over the raw edges.

4 Make a crease 4cm (1½in) from the top edge of the blind folding towards the wrong side. Machine stitch the creased edge in place 3cm (1¼in) down from the fold, to form the casing for the roller blind lath.

5 Lay the fabric right side up on a table. Using masking tape, carefully fix the other raw edge centrally along the roller tacking line, with the flat pin on the left. Carefully hammer in the tacks and roll up the blind (**D**).

6 Cut the top lath to 2cm (¾in) longer than the finished width of the blind, and slot it into the top casing. Fix the toggle holder to the centre of the lath casing, screwing through the fabric and lath on the wrong side of the blind (this will anchor the lath and stop it from slipping out at either end) (**E**).

7 Attach hooks to each side of the window frame, about halfway up the window but equidistant from the sill. Attach the remaining hooks about halfway down to the sill, one to each side. Clip the blind into the brackets, and tension it, following the instructions in the kit. To operate, pull up the blind and fix it in position, by slipping the lath ends over one of the two sets of hooks (**F**). An alternative way to hold this blind in place is to attach a strip of touch-and-close tape horizontally to your window frame, and stitch the corresponding side to the wrong side of the lath channel, so that when it is raised the touch-and-close tape grips it in place (the lath is not visible at each end of the channel if you use this method, and no hooks are required).

STUDDED LEATHER BLIND

Made from mock leather fabric, this unlined recess-fixed Roman blind is only very minimally stitched. The method for making an unlined Roman blind differs from that of a lined blind in that the rod pockets in an unlined blind are formed from folds in the main fabric of the blind.

MATERIALS
- Fabric (see below for estimating the quantity)
- Fabric glue
- Masking tape
- Matching thread
- Brass rings (three per rod pocket)
- 5 x 2.5cm (2 x 1in) timber support to fit the width of the window recess
- Decorative studs (to attach the blind to its support)
- Timber dowels for each rod pocket, 1cm (⅜in) in diameter and cut 5cm (2in) shorter than the finished width of the blind
- Four large screw eyes
- Fine cord
- Toggle end and cleat

ESTIMATING THE FABRIC

Measure your window (see page 120) to find out the finished length and width for a recess-fixed blind. Add 10cm (4in) to both the length and width measurements for hem allowances, and then turn to page 122 to work out exactly what quantity of fabric you will need for an unlined Roman blind.

MAKING THE BLIND

1 Cut out the blind fabric. Fold to the wrong side, and crease, hems 5cm (2in) deep around all edges. Mitre each corner by trimming away the hem fabric diagonally, then glue down the hems using fabric glue (**A**). Use masking tape to help you hold the hems in place as you work, and weight them down until the glue is completely dry.

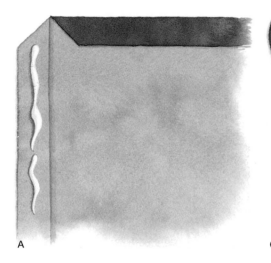

A

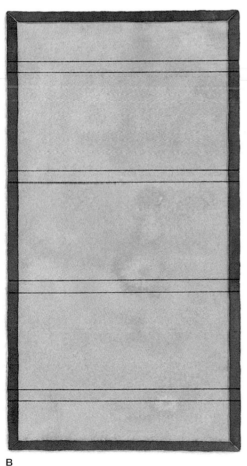

B

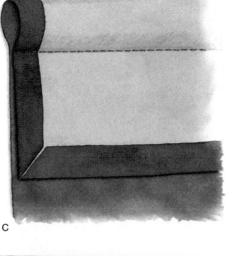

C

D

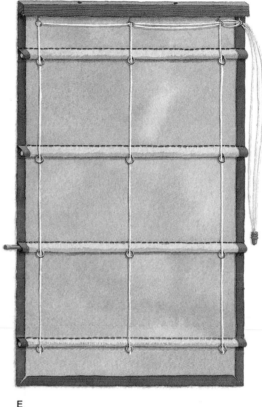

E

2 Measure up from the hem the pocket spacings that you worked out when estimating your fabric (see unlined Roman blind, page 123). Mark the 5cm (2in) wide rod pocket positions with tailor's chalk across the blind on the wrong side of the fabric (**B**).

3 With the right sides of fabric facing, fold the blind along the centre of one rod pocket, lining up the chalk lines. Using a special leather foot on your machine and a large machine stitch, stitch the pocket in place 2.5cm (1in) from the fold, reverse stitching at each end of the stitch-line to secure (**C**). You can use masking tape to hold the sides together as you stitch, in order to help prevent slippage. Repeat for the remaining rod pockets and brush away the chalk marks.

4 Hand-sew brass rings to the folded edge of each rod pocket. One should be positioned 5cm (2in) in from the outside edge of the the blind, and one centrally in between. Align all rings with those on the pockets above and below them.

5 Prepare the timber support (see page 121, ignoring references to touch-and-close tape). Fasten the top edge of the blind to the face of the support, by hammering the decorative studs in place close to the top edge, 2.5cm (1in) apart (**D**). Fix the timber support in place, by screwing it either to the ceiling of the window recess, or to the actual window frame, below the line of studs.

6 Insert a doweling rod into each pocket. If desired, slipstitch the pocket ends closed. Working from the back of the blind, knot a length of the fine cord to each of the bottom rings and thread the cord up through the rest of the rings. Thread the cords through the screw eyes directly above in the timber support, then pass the cords across so that they all pass through the fourth eye. Trim the cords level and attach the toggle to the ends (**E**).

7 Screw the cleat to the side of the window frame, so that you can secure the cords firmly when the blind is raised. Try to make sure that the cleat is not visible when the blind is raised.

BAY WINDOW BLINDS

These soft cotton lawn blinds are basically unlined Roman blinds without rods at the back. The rigid rods make a blind more formal, by keeping it very straight and flat. Omitting the rods creates a more casual effect, as the blind crumples up softly at the sides and swags down in the centre.

MATERIALS

- 5 x 2.5cm (2 x 1in) timber support to fit the width of the window recess
- Three large screw eyes
- Fabric (see below for estimating the quantity)
- Matching thread
- Brass rings (two for each folding position)
- Touch-and-close tape to fit the width of the finished blind
- Fine cord
- Toggle end and cleat

A

ESTIMATING THE FABRIC

Prepare the timber support for a recess-fixed blind as shown on page 121 (there are only two rows of cording rings for this blind), and fix in place. Measure your window (see page 120) to find out the finished length and width of the blind. Add 12cm (5in) to the length and width measurements for hem allowances. This blind is best made from one piece of fabric, but – as above – if you need more than one width, allow for a full fabric width to be placed centrally, with any part-widths of equal dimensions joined down each side.

MAKING THE BLIND

1 Cut out the required number of fabric drops and join the widths together, if necessary, with flat fell seams (see page 128). Press a double 3cm (1¼in) hem along the side edges and machine stitch in place close to the first fold. Turn and press the same hem along the lower edge and stitch In place as before. Slipstitch (see page 130) the open ends of the base hem together at the sides.

2 Work out the pocket spacing for the ring positions (see page 122). Working on the wrong side of the blind, measure up from the base hem the pocket spacing worked out and mark on the stitch line of the side hems with pins. Hand-sew brass rings to the inner edge of the side hems at the positions marked, for the two cording rows (**A**). Complete the blind following steps 9, 11 and 12 of the lined Roman blind (see page 126).

ROMAN BLIND & SHEERS

The Roman blind at this modern window has been softened by hanging a long sheer curtain in front. The fully lined Roman blind is set in the window recess and has a contrast fabric border down the sides and edges. The sheer curtain is a fixed dress curtain, with a triple-pleat heading formed by a heading tape hung from a track. The sheer is pulled back from the window to reveal the blind – by a large narrow fabric loop, caught around a hook at one side of the window.

MATERIALS

For the lined Roman blind:
- 5 x 2.5cm (2 x 1in) timber support to fit the width of the window recess
- Large screw eyes (approximately four, one for each cording row plus one extra)
- Main fabric, contrast fabric and lining (see below for estimating the quantities)
- Matching thread
- Brass rings (approximately three for each rod pocket, depending on the width of the blind)
- Touch-and-close tape to fit the width of the finished blind
- Timber dowels for each rod pocket, 1cm (⅜in) in diameter and cut 5cm (2in) shorter than the finished width of the blind
- Fine cord
- Toggle end and cleat

For the sheer curtain:
- Sheer fabric (see below for estimating the quantity)
- Matching thread
- Chain weight (optional)
- Deep triple-pleat heading tape, to fit the width of the ungathered curtain
- Cord tidy
- Metal two-prong curtain hooks

For the tieback:
- Sheer fabric (see below for estimating the quantity)
- Matching thread
- Tieback hook

A

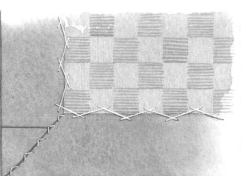

B

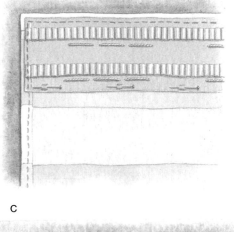

C

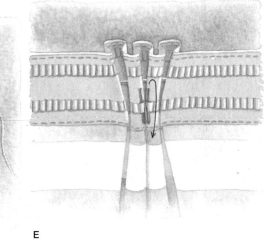

D

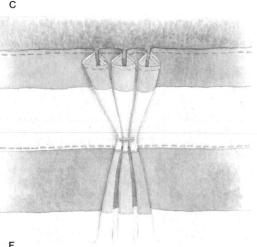

E

F

ESTIMATING THE FABRIC

For the Roman blind, prepare and fix the recess-fixed timber support (see page 121). Measure your window (see page 120) to find out the dimensions for a recess-fixed blind. For the main fabric, subtract 5cm (2in) from the width measurement. If you need more than one width of main fabric, the full fabric width should be placed centrally, with part-widths placed symmetrically down each side.

For the lining, do not add extra for hem allowances, but see page 122 for your quantity, allowing for a three-quarter depth rod pocket spacing at the base of the blind, to enable the border to remain visible below the folds when the blind is raised.

For the contrast borders, allow two side strips 15cm (6in) wide, and the same length as the finished length of the blind, and one base strip 15cm (6in) wide, and the finished width of the blind, plus 15cm (6in), long.

For the sheer curtain, face-fix your track in place and measure your window (see page 120), to find the finished width and length of your curtain. For

this style the curtain will need to hang from the centre row of pockets on the heading tape, to allow the track to be covered. For a triple-pleat heading you will need a fabric fullness of twice your measured curtain width. Add 20cm (8in) to the curtain length for hem allowances. Turn to page 122 to calculate your final fabric requirements.

For the tieback, allow for a straight-grain strip of sheer fabric 6cm (2½in) wide, and 1m (1¼yd) long.

MAKING THE ROMAN BLIND

1 Cut the required number of fabric and lining drops, and join the widths together, if necessary, with plain straight seams (see page 127). Stitch the two side borders to each side of the central part of the blind with plain straight seams, with a seam allowance of 2.5cm (1in). Press the seams open. Stitch the base border to the lower edge of the blind in the same way (**A**).

2 Press an 8cm (3in) hem to the wrong side down both sides and across the base of the blind. Mitre the lower corners on the wrong side (see page 128). Slipstitch the mitred edges together and stitch all the hems in place with large herringbone stitches (**B**). Continue to make up the blind following steps 2 to 12 of the lined Roman blind on page 125.

MAKING THE SHEER CURTAIN

1 Make the sheer curtain (see the unlined curtain instructions, page 123). Mark the finished length with pins. Press and pin the top hem to the wrong side. This will be concealed by the heading tape.

2 Cut the heading tape, allowing for an unpleated section at each end, plus 2.5cm (1in) for hems. From the leading edge, position the tape on the wrong side of the curtain, close to the top edge. Fold under 1.5cm (⅝in) at one end and secure. Pin in place, folding under a 1.5cm (⅝in) hem at the opposite end and leaving the cord ends free.

3 Starting at the lower edge of the tape on the leading edge, machine stitch up the short edge of the tape, along the top and down the opposite short edge (**C**). Again starting at the leading edge, machine stitch along the lower edge of the tape, ensuring that the fabric below is kept smooth, otherwise the curtain may pucker when the tape is pulled up. Remove the pins.

4 Pull up the cords evenly. Push the first set of pleats into position (**D**), move on to the second set, and push them into position. Then return to the first set, as they will have come undone, and continue along the length of the tape until all the pleats are pulled up. Knot the cord ends together and wind the loose ends around the cord tidy and secure in place. Do not cut off the excess cords, as this would mean that the curtains could not be pulled out flat for cleaning.

5 Fit the two-prong hooks into the back of each pleat. To do this, insert the two prongs from the underside, one into each of the adjacent hook pockets at the back of the pleats (**E**), and thread them through to face down towards the hem. Fit one hook to each end of the heading tape.

6 On the right side of the curtain, hand-stitch a small tack to the base of each pleat, to pinch the three pleats together and form a better fan shape (**F**). Hang the curtain from the track, fastening the first and last hooks through the end stop rings, to hold the curtain in place and prevent it from sliding along the track.

MAKING THE TIEBACK

With right sides together, fold the tieback strip in half lengthways, keeping the raw edges together. Stitch across one short end and along the long side. Snip the corners and then invert, to turn the strip right side out, using a knitting needle or similar object. Tuck the raw end into the tube and slipstitch the edges together. Tie the strip around the curtain and loop it over the tieback hook at the side of the window. Hide the tied ends behind the curtain, so that you only see the fabric loop.

DENIM BLIND & CURTAIN

A blind combined with a curtain is used here very effectively for a child's room. The fully-lined Roman blind is hung in the window recess and decorated along the lower edge with denim pockets, ideal for storing little items.

The curtain hung in front is fully interlined. Making an interlined curtain requires a fair amount of skill, and involves handling large areas of fabric and interlining, but the effort is well worth it. The result is a wonderful thick curtain that hangs beautifully, is draught-proof and gives a total blackout to the room when drawn.

In contrast, no effort whatsoever is required for making the tieback. Take a couple of children's elasticated snake belts and simply fasten them around the curtain at the right height. To complete the window, the track and fixings are all concealed by a fabric-covered box pelmet.

Materials

For the interlined curtains:

- Main fabric, lining, and bump or domette interlining (see below for estimating the quantities)
- Matching thread
- Curtain weights (optional)
- Pencil-pleat heading tape, to fit the width of the ungathered curtain
- Cord tidy

For the lined Roman blind:

- 5 x 2.5cm (2 x 1in) timber support to fit the width of the window recess
- Four large screw eyes
- Fabric and lining (see below for estimating quantities)
- Matching thread
- Touch-and-close tape to fit the width of the finished blind
- Pairs of old denim jeans for the back pockets (optional)
- Brass rings (approximately three per rod pocket, depending on the width of the blind)
- Timber dowels for each rod pocket, 1cm (⅜in) in diameter and cut 5cm (2in) shorter than the finished width of the blind
- Fine cord
- Toggle end and cleat

A

For the box pelmet:

- Fabric, lining and bump or domette interlining
- Matching thread
- Buckram or other stiffener, the same size as the finished pelmet, including returns (see page 122 for measuring up)
- Fabric glue
- Touch-and-close tape to fit the length of the finished pelmet, including returns
- 25–30cm (10–12in) deep pelmet board, fitted in place (see page 121)

ESTIMATING THE FABRIC

For the interlined curtain, fix your track in place to the underside of the pelmet board and measure your window (see page 120) for the dimensions of your curtain. For a pencil-pleat heading, you will need a fabric fullness of 2½–3 times your measured curtain width. Add 20cm (8in) to the curtain length for hem allowances, then turn to page 122 to work out how much fabric you require.

For the Roman blind, prepare the timber support (see page 121), and fix in place. Measure your window (see page 120) to establish the dimensions for a recess-fixed blind. Add 10cm (4in) for hem allowances to the length and width measurements of the main fabric, but do not add anything to the lining. Instead, see page 122 to work out your quantity, allowing for a full-depth rod pocket spacing at the base of the blind to ensure that the pockets remain visible when the blind is raised.

Turn to page 122 to work out the fabric, lining and interlining quantities required for the pelmet.

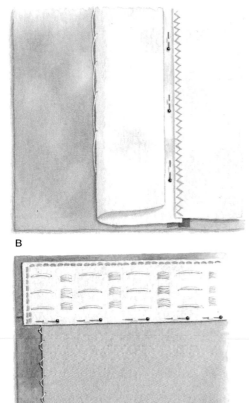

B

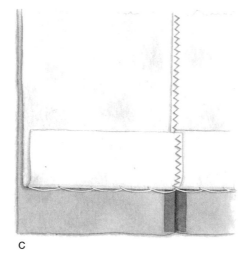

C

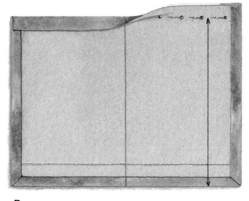

D

E

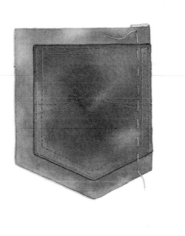

F

G

MAKING THE INTERLINED CURTAIN

1 Cut out the fabric, interlining and lining drops, and join pieces as necessary, using lapped seams to join the interlining pieces.

2 Lay the fabric face down, interlining on top. Pin together along the seam nearest the leading edge. Halfway between this seam and the leading edge pin the interlining to the fabric again (**A**).

3 Fold back the interlining to the half-width pin-line. Starting 15cm (6in) up from the hem edge, use large locking stitches 10cm (4in) apart, to secure the lining to the main fabric (**B**).

4 Fold the interlining back over the fabric and smooth. Pin the layers together down the leading edge, 5cm (2in) in from the raw edges. Fold the interlining back again to this new pin-line and secure to the fabric with locking stitches as before.

5 Move across to the original pinned seam and lock the layers together down the seam turnings. Continue across the curtain as before, making the last row 5cm (2in) in from the outer edge.

6 Pin the interlining to the fabric 15cm (6in) up from the hem edge. Fold back the interlining to the pin-line and lock the layers together (**C**). The main fabric and lining are now locked together and can be made up as one piece of fabric. To complete the curtain, follow the instructions for the lined curtain from step 2 (see page 124).

7 After marking the finished length of the curtain with pins, press the top hem over to the wrong side along the pin-line (**D**). This hem allowance will be concealed by the heading tape, so if there is too much, just trim some away.

8 Starting at the leading edge, position the heading tape on the wrong side of the curtain, close to the top edge. Fold under 1.5cm (⅝in) of tape at one end and secure on the wrong side of the tape. Pin the tape in place. Cut the tape at the other end, allowing 1.5cm (⅝in) for folding under.

9 Starting at the lower edge of the tape on the leading edge, machine stitch up the short edge of the tape, along the top and down the opposite short edge (**E**). Starting again at the leading edge, machine stitch along the lower edge of the tape, ensuring that the fabric below is kept smooth.

10 Pull up the cords until the finished curtain width is established and then knot the ends together. Wind the loose ends around the cord tidy. Do not cut off the excess cords (to allow the curtains to be pulled out flat for cleaning). Arrange the pleats evenly and hang the curtains from the inner track.

MAKING THE ROMAN BLIND AND BOX PELMET

Make the blind following steps 1 to 9 of the lined Roman blind instructions (see page 125). To attach the decorative denim pockets, cut out the back pockets from old pairs of jeans, leaving a 2.5cm (1in) hem allowance around all the sides. Press the hems to the wrong side and tack in place (**F**). Pin the pockets to the lower part of the blind on the right side below the first rod pocket and slipstitch in place around all the edges (**G**). Continue making the blind according to the instructions for lined Roman blind from step 10 (see page 126).

Make up the pelmet following the box pelmet instructions on page 127.

NIGHT & DAY CURTAINS

To create this look, gauzy sheers are hung in front of a pair of fully-lined taffeta curtains, giving a modern twist to what is a traditional theme. The curtains can be used separately or together to create various moods. The tracks are then concealed by a neat fabric-covered box pelmet.

MATERIALS

For the lined curtains:
- Main fabric and lining (see below for estimating the quantities)
- Matching thread
- Curtain weights (optional)
- Pencil-pleat heading tape, to fit the width of the ungathered curtain
- Cord tidy

For the sheers:
- Sheer fabric (see below for estimating the quantity)
- Matching thread
- Chain weight (optional)
- Lightweight pencil-pleat heading tape, to fit the width of the ungathered curtain

For the box pelmet:
- Fabric, lining and bump or domette interlining
- Matching thread
- Buckram or other stiffener, the same size as the finished pelmet, including returns (see page 122 for measuring up)
- Fabric glue
- Touch-and-close tape to fit the length of the finished pelmet, including returns
- 25–30cm (10–12in) deep pelmet board, fitted in place (see page 121)

ESTIMATING THE FABRICS

For the curtains, fix two tracks to the underside of your pelmet board and measure your window (see page 120) to establish the dimensions of your curtains. You will need fabric 2½–3 times your measured curtain width for both the sheer and the lined curtain as both have a pencil-pleat heading.

For the lined curtains, add 20cm (8in) to the curtain length for hem allowances at the top and base, then turn to page 122 to work out how much fabric, lining and sheer fabric you will need.

For the pelmet, turn to page 122 to work out the fabric, lining and interlining quantities required.

MAKING THE LINED CURTAINS

1 Make the lined curtains following the instructions on page 124. Having marked the length with pins, press the top hem over to the wrong side along the pin-line (**A**). This allowance will be concealed, so trim it if there is too much.

2 Starting at the leading edge, position the heading tape on the wrong side of the curtain, close to the top edge. Fold under about 1.5cm (⅝in) of tape at one end and secure the cords with a knot on the wrong side of the tape. Pin the tape in place. Allowing a further 1.5cm (⅝in) for folding under, cut off the heading tape at the opposite end, and leave the cord ends free.

3 Starting at the lower edge of the tape on the leading edge, machine stitch up the short edge of the tape, along the top and down the opposite short edge (**B**). Starting again at the leading edge, machine stitch along the lower edge of the tape, ensuring that the fabric below is smooth, otherwise the curtain may pucker when the tape is pulled up.

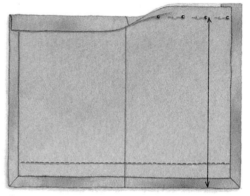

A

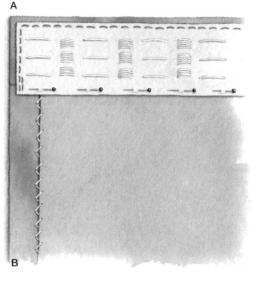

B

4 Pull up the cords evenly to the finished curtain width required and knot the cord ends together. Wind the loose ends around the cord tidy and secure in place. Do not cut off the excess cords, as this would mean that the curtains ccould not be pulled out flat for cleaning. Arrange the pleats evenly and hang the curtains from the inner track.

MAKING THE SHEERS AND BOX PELMET

Make the sheers, following the unlined curtain instructions on page 123. Then attach the heading tape to the top edge of the sheer curtains as shown above and hang them from the outer track in front of the lined curtains from the outer track.

Make up the pelmet following the box pelmet instructions on page 127.

GREEN FABRIC SHUTTER

Made from a flat piece of heavy-weight double-sided silk fabric, this simple shutter is threaded on to a hinged curtain rod at the top. The fabric used here is a different colour on each side, but you could easily achieve the same effect by using a contrasting coloured fabric as a lining. A complementary coloured silk has been used as a binding on all four edges of the shutter.

MATERIALS

- Brass hinged curtain rod
- Main double-sided fabric (or main fabric and a contrasting fabric for the lining), and contrast binding fabric (see below for estimating the quantities)
- Matching thread

ESTIMATING THE FABRIC

Face-fix the hinged curtain rod to the top of the window, at one side. To find out the finished width and length of your shutter, measure the window length from the top of the rod to the floor, and for the width, the length of the rod arm. This style is best made from one piece of fabric; add 1.5cm (⅝in) to the shutter length for a hem allowance at the top, but nothing to the width.

If you are lining your banner with a fabric in a contrasting colour, allow for a piece the same size as the main banner fabric.

For the side bindings, allow for two straight grain strips in contrast fabric, 15cm (6in) wide, and the length of the finished shutter, plus a 1.5cm (⅝in) hem allowance. For the base binding, allow for a straight-grain strip in a contrasting fabric, 15cm (6in) wide, and the finished width of the shutter, plus 3cm (1¼in) for hem allowances. For the top binding, allow a straight-grain strip 13cm (5¼in) wide, and the finished width of the shutter, plus 5cm (2in) for hem allowances.

MAKING THE SHUTTER

1 If using a separate lining, tack the two main pieces together around all edges, wrong sides facing, and make up as if it is one piece of fabric. With wrong sides together, fold the side and base binding strips in half lengthways, keeping raw edges together, and press. Starting at the top, place one of the doubled side binding pieces on to the right side of the shutter at the leading edge, keeping the raw edges level. Machine stitch the binding in place with a 4cm (1½in) seam allowance.

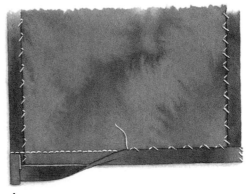

A

2 Fold the binding over on to the back of the shutter, and slipstitch the folded edge of the binding in place just covering the machine stitches. Repeat steps 1 and 2 with the other side edge and binding.

3 Attach the binding to the base as per step 1, allowing the short ends of the binding to extend 1.5cm (⅝in) at each side. Turn back the short ends of the binding level with the side edges of the shutter and press. Then complete the binding process following step 2 (**A**). Slipstitch the open binding ends together at the base side edges.

B

4 Turn over a double 1.5cm (⅝in) hem to the wrong side at each short end of the top binding strip, and slipstitch the hems in place. With right sides together, place the binding on to the shutter at the top, keeping the raw edges level, and the short hemmed ends level with the shutter sides. Machine stitch the binding in place with a 4cm (1½in) seam allowance (**B**).

5 Press a 1.5cm (⅝in) hem to the wrong side on the remaining edge of the top binding. Fold the binding on to the back of the shutter, and slipstitch the pressed edge in place just covering the machine stitches. Work a row of machine stitches 1.5cm (⅝in) down from the top folded edge, to form a channel for the curtain rod in the binding (**C**). Slip the shutter on to the curtain rod to complete.

C

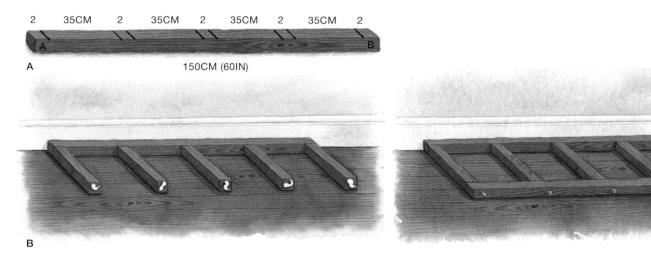

STANDING SCREEN

In this project a screen is used in conjunction with a fully lined Roman blind as an unusual window dressing. Both the beautiful maple screen with transparent hinges and the polypropylene screen featured are made to order (see page 159 for stockist details). Alternatively, you can make your own screen using wooden panels, or a framework with sheer fabric stretched across. You do not have to be a clever carpenter to make them, as long as you can use a screwdriver and hammer, and provided the wood is cut to size for you by a timber merchant so that the ends are exactly square.

MATERIALS

For the covered frame screen:
- Six pieces of 2cm (¾in) square, planed finished timber, 1.5m (5ft) long
- Fifteen pieces of 2cm (¾in) square, planed finished timber, 40cm (16in) long
- Wood glue
- 3.5cm (1½in) long oval nails
- Toning emulsion paint
- 6.5m (7¼yd) of sheer fabric, 120cm (48in) wide
- Approximately 400 flat-headed tacks, 1cm (⅜in) long
- 12m (13yd) of vinyl tape 1.5cm (⅝in) wide, and white upholstery tacks, or braid and flat-headed tacks (optional)
- Six brass or chrome hinges, 2 x 6cm (¾ x 2½in)
- Brass or chrome screws for hinges

For the wooden panel screen:
- Three wooden or medium-density fibreboard (MDF) panels, 150 x 44cm (60 x 17in)
- If using MDF, paint or wallpaper to cover the panels
- If using wallpaper, strong spray glue
- If using wooden panels, varnish
- Six brass or chrome hinges, 2 x 6cm (¾ x 2½in)
- Brass or chrome screws for the hinges

For the lined Roman blind:
- 5 x 2.5cm (2 x 1in) timber support to fit the width of the window recess
- Four large screw eyes
- Fabric and lining (see below for estimating quantities)
- Matching thread
- Brass rings (approximately three per rod pocket, depending on the width of the blind)
- Touch-and-close tape to fit the width of the finished blind
- Timber dowels for each rod pocket, 1cm (⅜in) in diameter and cut 5cm (2in) shorter than the finished width of the blind
- Fine cord
- Toggle end and cleat

ESTIMATING THE BLIND FABRIC

For the Roman blind, prepare the timber support for a face-fixed blind as shown on page 121, and fix in place. Measure your window (see page 120) to find out the finished length and width of the blind. For the main fabric, add 10cm (4in) to both the length and width measurements for hem allowances. For the lining, do not add extra for hem allowances, but turn to page 122 to work out your final fabric requirement.

MAKING THE COVERED FRAME SCREEN

1 Take one of the timber uprights and, using a set square, pencil in the positions where the horizontals will be attached, as shown (**A**). Mark the top and the base of the uprights on the ends. To ensure that all the uprights are marked in exactly the same places, line up the remaining five next to the first, and repeat the markings on them.

2 Place one upright on the floor against a wall with the markings towards you. Place the horizontals in position, checking with a set square that they are correctly aligned. Smear glue on to the outward-facing ends of the horizontals (**B**).

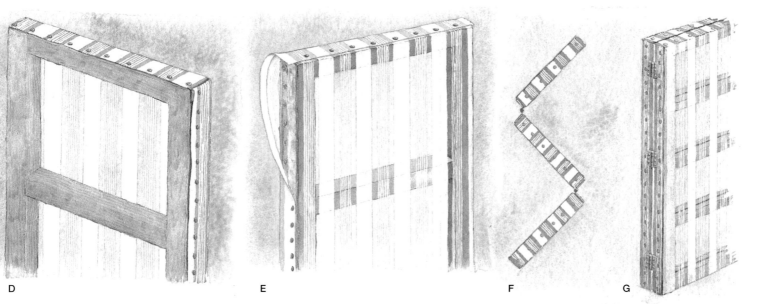

D   E   F   G

3 Take another upright and knock an oval nail into the centre of each marking until the points just begin to show through on the other side of the timber. Place this upright against the horizontals, matching up the nails with the centre of each horizontal (**C**). Hammer them home, starting with the middle one, then the ones at each end, and then finally the remaining two. Wipe off any excess glue with a clean, damp cloth.

4 Turn the frame around so that the nailed upright is now against the wall and smear glue on the opposite ends of the horizontals. Knock nails into the second upright as before. Place the upright against the glued horizontals, checking that the marks correspond, and hammer the nails home. Leave to dry overnight. Make up two more frames following steps 1 to 4. Paint all the frames with emulsion paint and leave to dry.

5 Cut out three rectangles of sheer fabric to fit the size of a single frame, plus an extra 2cm (¾in) hem allowance all the way around, and another three with an extra 3.5cm (1½in) hem allowance all the way around. The quickest way to do this is to lay the fabric out on the floor, right side up, place the frames on top, and mark the hem allowances with tailor's chalk. In this way, you can see exactly how any prints or patterns match up on each frame before you cut out the fabric.

6 Place one frame on a flat surface, lay one of the smaller fabric pieces (with the smaller hem allowances) centrally on top, right side up. To secure it, start by knocking in a holding tack at the centre of the top edge. Pull gently on the fabric so that it is taut and secure with a holding tack at the centre of the bottom edge. Secure the sides in the same way. These holding tacks should only be knocked in lightly, then removed after step 7 has been completed.

7 Stand the frame upright and fold the fabric over. Secure with tacks, about 12cm (5in) apart. Do not tack the corners yet. Turn the screen the other way up, pulling the fabric so that it feels firm, but not stretched. Repeat to attach the fabric at the two sides. Fold the corners neatly and tack in place. Trim away any excess fabric that overhangs the back of the frame (**D**).

8 Lay the covered frame fabric side down and place one of the larger fabric pieces centrally on top, right side up, and knock in holding tacks in the centre of each side as shown in step 6.

9 Stand the frame upright once again, and fold the raw fabric edge under along the top edge so that it is flush with the front of the frame. Secure the top edge in place with tacks, as described in step 7. Repeat to secure the remaining sides (**E**). Attach braid or vinyl tape around the outer edges of the panel, using upholstery tacks, to disguise the flat-headed tacks. Repeat steps 6 to 9 to cover the two remaining frames.

10 Place two of the covered panels together so that the tops and bases correspond. Mark the positions of the three hinges on the side edges of each screen. Remove one or two of the upholstery tacks with a blunt knife for the hinge screws. Screw the hinges loosely in position, and then stand the panels up to check the positioning (**G**), before tightening up the screws. Hinge the remaining panel so that the screen concertinas (**F**).

MAKING THE WOODEN PANEL SCREEN

Paint, varnish, or cover your panels with wallpaper. Then screw the hinges in place, as described in step 10 of the covered frame screen, but ignoring references to tacks.

MAKING THE ROMAN BLIND

Make the blind, following the lined Roman blind instructions on page 125.

A

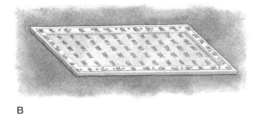

B

C

D

SHEER DOOR PANEL

This screen has been made very simply by stretching sheer fabric on to an MDF framework. The frame is then hinged at the side, and fastened to either a window frame for privacy, or to a wall as a room divider. Because it is hinged at the side, it can be swung out of the way when not required.

MATERIALS

- Two pieces of 7cm x 6mm (3 x ¼in) MDF, the height of the frame, and two pieces the width of the frame (see below for estimating quantities)
- Two pieces of 7 x 2cm (3 x ¾in) MDF the height of the frame, and two pieces the width of the frame (see below for estimating quantities)
- Sheer fabric (see below for estimating quantity)
- Strong wood glue
- Toning coloured emulsion, or eggshell finish paint
- Approximately 100 flat-headed tacks, 1cm (⅜in) long
- Sixteen oval nails, 2cm (¾in) long
- Woodfiller
- Fine sandpaper
- 5 x 2.5cm (2 x 1in) timber fixing batten, the height of the panel, plus 2.5cm (1in) for clearance
- Three brass or chrome hinges, 2cm (¾in) wide and 6cm (2½in) long
- Brass or chrome screws for hinges

ESTIMATING THE MATERIALS

Measure your window, and decide on the finished size of your screen. Remember that the screen will be face-fixed in place with the timber batten at the side of the window, so take into account any skirting board and windowsills that may affect the positioning of the screen and batten. For the top frame, allow for two upright pieces of the 6mm (¼in) thick MDF equal to the finished height of the frame, and two horizontal pieces equal to the width, minus 14cm (5½in).

For the under-frame, allow for two upright pieces of the 2cm (¾in) thick MDF equal to the finished height of the frame, minus 14cm (5½in), and two horizontal pieces equal to the finished width of the frame. Get your timber merchant to cut the MDF to size, so that the ends are square.

The sheer fabric to cover the panel needs to be the finished height and width of the screen, with 2cm (¾in) subtracted from both measurements.

MAKING THE SCREEN

1 Lay one of the thick MDF uprights flat on the floor against a wall. Smear strong glue on one end of each of the thick horizontals, and stick them to each end of the upright. Smear more glue on the opposite end of the horizontals and place the second thick upright against the ends to make the frame. Wipe off excess glue and dry overnight (**A**). When the glue has dried, paint the frame and remaining pieces of MDF, and leave to dry.

2 Cut out a rectangle of sheer fabric to fit the frame, minus 1cm (⅜in) all the way around. To do this lay the fabric on the floor, right side up, and place the frame on top of it. Mark around the edge with tailor's chalk. Cut out the fabric, following a line 1cm (⅜in) inside the chalk line.

3 Place the frame on a flat surface and lay the fabric piece centrally on top, right side facing. To secure it to the frame, knock in a holding tack at the centre of the top edge. Pull on the fabric gently so it is taut and secure with a holding tack at the centre bottom. Secure the sides in the same way.

4 Secure the fabric at the top and base with a series of tacks, spaced at about 12cm (5in) intervals, pulling the fabric so that it feels firm and taut, but not stretched. Repeat to attach the fabric at the two sides of the frame (**B**). Remove the holding tacks (see step 3). Neatly trim away any excess fabric that overhangs the frame.

5 Smear glue on to the wrong side of the thinner MDF horizontals and place them on top of the frame, covering the fabric raw edges and tacks. Smear glue on to the wrong side of the remaining two uprights and place them in between the horizontals, again covering the fabric raw edges and tacks, and keeping the edges level.

6 Nail the upper frame to the lower frame, positioning one nail centrally at each corner of the frame, one in the centre halfway down each upright and one centrally halfway along each horizontal (**C**). Wipe off any excess glue with a clean, damp cloth and leave to dry overnight. When dry, turn the frame over and hammer extra nails centrally at each end of the horizontals. Fill the nail-heads with woodfiller, if required. When dry, rub lightly with sandpaper and paint over the nail-heads.

7 Paint the timber fixing batten to match your décor. When dry, screw it to the wall. Screw the hinges loosely in position to the back of the frame along the upright, stand the sheer door panel up against the batten to ensure the correct positioning and tighten up the screws. Screw the opposite side of the hinges to the timber batten, keeping the top edges level and leaving 2.5cm (1in) for clearance at the base (**D**).

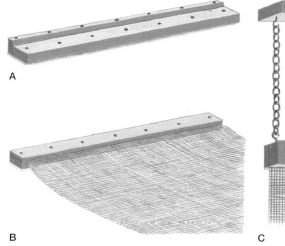

A

B

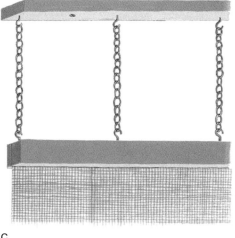

C

MESH SCREEN

These room-dividing screens are rather like large fixed roller blinds. The ones featured have been professionally made to order (see page 159 for stockist details). Alternatively, you can make your own, providing that you can get hold of a pre-stiffened fabric that is sufficiently wide. Each mesh screen is supported by a timber framework at the top and base, and suspended from the ceiling with chrome chains.

MATERIALS

- 5 x 2.5cm (2 x 1in) timber ceiling fixing batten, the width of the screen
- Two pieces of 4 x 2cm (1½ x ¾in) MDF or timber, the width of the screen
- Two pieces of 4cm x 6mm (1½ x ¼in) MDF or timber, the width of the screen
- Toning coloured emulsion, or eggshell finish paint
- Pre-stiffened roller blind fabric (see below for estimating the quantity)
- Approximately 100 flat-headed tacks, 1cm (⅜in) long
- Strong wood glue
- Oval nails, 2cm (¾in) long
- Woodfiller
- Fine sandpaper
- Large chrome cup hooks for the top of the screen, and corresponding ones for the timber fixing batten
- Chrome chain (allow for 25cm (10in) of chain for each set of hooks)

ESTIMATING THE FABRIC

Measure the height of your room from floor to ceiling and subtract 35cm (14in) for the chain fixings. The width of your screen will depend on the width of your fabric, as pre-stiffened fabric cannot be joined together very satisfactorily. Instead, if you need a larger screen, make several smaller screens and hang them side by side.

MAKING THE SCREEN

1 Paint all the timber pieces on all sides, and leave them to dry. Take the ceiling fixing batten and, using a pencil, mark the hook positions down the centre on one wide face, spacing them approximately 25cm (10in) apart, and placing the first and the last one 2.5cm (1in) in from the ends. To ensure that the top frame is marked in exactly the same places, line up one of the thick timber pieces next to the ceiling fixing batten, with one of its narrow sides on top, and transfer the markings. With a bradawl, prepare the holes for hooks on both the top frame and ceiling fixing batten (**A**).

2 Place the top timber piece with the prepared holes on the floor, with a wide face down and the holes facing away from you. Lay the top edge of the fabric right side up on to the timber, with its long edge 1cm (⅜in) in from the timber edge with the holes, and the side edges level with the timber ends. Secure the fabric in place with tacks, about 12cm (5in) apart, pulling the fabric so that it feels firm, but not stretched. Repeat to attach the fabric to the remaining thick timber piece at the base.

3 Smear glue on to the wrong side of the thinner timber strips and place them on top of the thicker timber strips, covering the fabric raw edges and tacks, and ensuring that the edges are level with the lower frame.

4 Nail the upper frame to the lower frame, positioning the nails centrally along the timber, spaced approximately 25cm (10in) apart (**B**). Wipe off any excess glue with a clean, damp cloth and leave to dry overnight. Fill over the nail-heads if necessary with woodfiller. When dry, lightly rub the frame with sandpaper, and paint over the nail-heads.

5 Screw the hooks into the ceiling fixing batten and then drill some fixing holes centrally along the batten. Screw it in place to the ceiling. Hang a length of chain from each hook. Screw the remaining hooks into the top frame, and then get someone to support the screen, while you hook it on to the ends of the chains (**C**).

GLOSSARY

• **Appliqué:** The application of a layer of fabric in a design to a base cloth, using decorative stitching.

• **Architrave:** A decorative wooden surround to a door or window frame or around an arch.

• **Batten:** See Lath.

• **Bay window:** A window that projects from a wall to form an alcove.

• **Binding:** A strip of fabric, either straight-grain or bias (cut on the diagonal). Can be used to bind edges or for piping.

• **Blackout lining:** A special lining which blocks out all light.

• **Bow window:** A bay window shaped in a curve.

• **Bracket:** A decorative wooden or metal support which like a tieback holds a curtain back. Also, a means of attaching and supporting a shelf in position.

• **Bradawl:** A pointed tool used for making holes in a timber support.

• **Braid:** Woven yarns for trimming curtains, pelmets and tiebacks.

• **Brocade:** A heavy fabric, woven to create raised patterns. Traditionally made from silk, modern versions are now made from other yarns. The term has now come to mean any fabric with a raised pattern.

• **Buckram:** Stiffened hessian fabric used to give a permanent shape to tiebacks and pelmets. Fusible buckram is also available, which can be stuck to the fabric with the heat of an iron.

• **Bump:** A soft, blanket-like fabric used as interlining.

• **Calico:** A raw, unbleached cotton with a plain weave.

• **Cased heading:** A type of heading in which a channel is created in the fabric and is left open at both ends to receive a pole or rod.

• **Chintz:** Glazed cotton in plain colours or prints, suitable for curtains, blinds, pelmets and drapes. Must be dry-cleaned or the glaze will wash out.

• **Cleat:** A double-pronged hook which secures the cords of a blind.

• **Cornice:** A decorative plaster moulding that runs around the walls below the ceiling.

• **Daisy chain stitch:** See stitches, page 130.

• **Damask:** A fabric with a special weave that produces a raised pattern and a flat background. Damask can be made from many yarns.

• **Domette:** A soft, fine blanket layer material used as interlining. Thinner than bump.

• **Dormer window:** A window that projects from a sloping roof.

• **Dowel rod:** A slender wooden rod that is inserted into fabric pockets at the back of a blind, enabling it to be pulled up in neat folds.

• **Eyelet:** A two-part metal ring used as a heading for curtains and blinds.

• **Face-fixed:** Fixing blinds and curtains outside the window recess.

• **Facing:** A strip of fabric used to hide the raw edges of the main fabric.

• **Finial:** A decorative fixture attached to the ends of a curtain pole.

• **Finished drop:** The length of the finished curtain when hung.

• **Finished width:** The measurement from side edge to side edge once the curtain is gathered or pleated up.

• **Flat fell seam:** See seams, page 127.

• **French pleats:** Or Triple pleats. A curtain heading with three pleats separated by flat areas, formed by hand or tape.

• **French seam:** See seams, page 127.

• **Fringe:** A decorative edging with hanging threads or tassels.

• **Grain:** The direction in which the threads run in a woven fabric.

• **Heading:** The finishing at the top of a curtain or blind. Produced either by using tapes or by hand.

• **Hem:** The base edge of a curtain or blind, which is usually turned under and stitched in place.

• **Herringbone stitch:** See stitches, page 130.

• **Holland:** A hard-wearing cotton fabric, stiffened with oil or shellac. Used for pelmets and blinds.

• **Interfacing:** A stiffening fabric that is either stitched or ironed on.

• **Interlining:** A soft, but thick blanket-like fabric that adds bulk and improves the hang and insulation properties of curtains, pelmets and blinds. Often known as bump or domette.

• **Ladder stitch:** See stitches, page 129.

• **Lambrequin:** An ornamental hanging covering the upper part of a window or door, or the edge of a shelf.

• **Lapped seam:** See seams, page 128.

• **Lath:** Or batten. A flat piece of timber that slots into the base hem of a roller blind so that the fabric hangs straight.

• **Lawn:** A fine cotton fabric, often used for children's dresses.

• **Leading edge:** The side edge of the curtain that will be at the centre when the curtains are closed. Or, on a single curtain, the edge that you draw across.

• **Lining:** Plain cotton or satin weave fabric. It protects curtains from light, and improves hanging and insulation.

• **Locking stitch:** See stitches, page 130.

• **Mitreing:** See basic techniques, page 128.

• **Muslin:** A fine gauzy cotton fabric.

• **Ombra:** A straight shaft that extends from the wall with a boss on the front over which a curtain may be draped.

• **Patchwork:** A fabric produced by stitching lots of small pieces of fabric together, usually in a decorative design.

• **Pelmet:** A stiffened shape running across the top of a window, used ornamentally and to hide the curtain track.

• **Pelmet board:** A horizontal board used to support the pelmet.

• **Pencil-pleat heading:** A curtain heading formed by hand or with a tape which creates a row of densely packed narrow folds.

• **Piping:** Fabric-covered piping cord used to emphasize the edges of curtains and tiebacks.

• **Recessed window:** A window set back into a wall. You can hang a curtain or blind inside it.

• **Return:** The part of a curtain or blind heading that turns around the end of the track, pelmet board or support.

• **Sash window:** Window that opens vertically by means of sash cords.

• **Satin:** A silk, cotton or synthetic fabric with a smooth, glossy surface and a dull back. Suitable for curtains, blinds, pelmets and drapes.

• **Seam allowance:** The narrow strip of raw-edged fabric left after making a seam, to allow for fraying.

• **Selvedges:** The tightly woven edge down both side edges of a fabric.

• **Silk noil:** A waste product of spun silk, which is mixed with cotton or wool to produce a fabric with added brilliance to the yarn.

• **Slipstitch:** See stitches, page 130.

• **Support:** A device such as a pole, track or batten from which a curtain or blind can be hung.

• **Taffeta:** A plain-weave fabric, made from silk or acetate, with a reflective sheen. Dry-clean only.

• **Tapestry:** A heavy, machine-woven fabric, that imitates the look of hand-woven tapestries.

• **Tartan:** A Scottish fabric made from wool or worsted, available in a variety of checks and colour ways.

• **Template:** A shape made from card or paper which is used as a pattern to mark outlines on fabric.

• **Ticking:** A strong, stiff fabric in a twill weave with a warp stripe.

• **Tieback hook:** A hook screwed to the wall, used to hold the rings or cords of a tieback.

• **Toile de Jouy:** A cotton fabric originally made in Jouy and printed in one colour with pastoral scenes.

• **Track:** Metal or plastic runners from which a curtain is hung.

• **Tweed:** A rough, robust, woollen fabric in a plain weave.

• **Velvet:** A luxurious fabric with a soft thick pile, made from cotton, silk or synthetic fibres.

• **Voile:** A light, plain-weave cotton, silk or polyester fabric.

• **Weave:** The interlacing action of yarns to form a fabric.

• **Weights:** See basic techniques, page 129.

• **Width of fabric:** The width measured from selvedge to selvedge. Most furnishing fabrics come in widths of either 122cm (48in) or 137cm (54in).

• **Worsted:** A smooth woollen fabric made from twisted yarn.

SUPPLIERS

FABRICS

Creation Baumann
41–42 Berners St
London W1P 3AA
Tel: 020 7637 0253
www.creationb.com
Available at Heals, Harrods
(Including Roll-up
Roll-down Blinds fabric
p.70–71)

Holland and Sherry
9–10 Saville Row
London WIX 1AF
Tel: 020 7437 0404
Phone for stockists. Wools
(Including Country Flannel
Curtain fabric p.28–29)

Hunter & Winterbotham
Bankfield Mills
St Mary's Lane, Bankfield
Tel: 020 7437 1425
haw@dial.pipex.com
Phone for stockists
(Including Suiting &
Satin curtain and blind
fabric p.34–35)

Jab International
1–15/16 Chelsea Harbour
Design Centre
London SW10 0XE
Tel: 020 7349 9323
www.jab.de/en
Phone for stockists/
wholesale only. Decorative
fabrics, voiles (Including
Wall of Silk curtain fabric
p.30–31; Long White
Sheer fabric p.56–57)

Mary Fox Linton Limited
1/9–10 Chelsea Harbour
Design Centre
London SW10 0XE
Tel: 020 7351 9908
(Including Blind fabric
p.6–7, p.74–75, p.82–83;
Edging fabric p.28–29;

Curtain fabric p.50–51,
p.82–83, p.88–89,
p.98–99; Sheer fabric
p.82–83, p.88–89,
p.102–103)

Nobilis
211 Chambers
Chelsea Harbour
Design Centre
London SW10 0XE
Tel: 020 7351 7878
Phone for stockists.
(Including Denim Blind &
Curtain fabric p.84–85)

Nya Nordiska
2/26 Chelsea Harbour
Design Centre
London SW10 0XE
Tel: 020 7351 2783
export@nya.de.fabric
Public welcome, design
service available.
(Including Silver Beaded
Sheers fabric p.58–59)

Ramm Son & Crocker
Chelsea Harbour
Design Centre
London SW10 0XE
Tel: 020 7352 093
Tel: 01494 446 555
sales@ramm.co.uk
Phone for stockists
(Including Bright Stripes
fabric p.46–47)

Sahco Hesslein
24 Chelsea Harbour
Design Centre
London SW10 0XE
Tel: 020 7352 6168
london@sachohesslein.com
www.sahco-hesslein.com
Public welcome. Fabric,
cushions (Including Silver
Beaded Sheers fabric
p.58–59)

Jim Thompson
1/8 Chelsea Harbour
Design Centre
London SW10 1XE
Tel: 020 7351 2829
(Including p.20; blind
fabric p.30–31; Curtain
fabric p.38–39, p.42–43,
p.96–97)

Whaleys Limited
Harris Court
Great Hoxton, Bradford
West Yorkshire BD7 4EQ
Tel: 01274 576718
info@whaleys.bradford.ltd.uk
www.whaleysbradford.ltd.uk
Drapes, curtains, textile
and garden bags.
(Including Bay Window
Blinds fabric p.76–77)

Zimmer Rhode
15 Chelsea Harbour
Design Centre
London SW10 0XE
Tel: 020 7351 7115
zimmer@z-r.co.uk
www.zr-group.com
Phone for stockists.
(Including Bright Stripes
fabric p.46–47; Hooked
Panel Blind p.66–67)

CURTAIN EDGING

Lelievre
1/19 Chelsea Harbour
Design Centre
London SW10 0XE
Tel: 020 7352 4798
www.lelievre-tissus.com
Decorative fabrics for
interior designers and
architects (Including
Suiting & Satin curtain
edging p.34–35)

See also **Mary Fox
Linton Limited**
(Including Country
Flannel Curtain edging
p.28–29)

TIEBACKS

Christina Ojo
Design Studio, Studio 1
14 Porchester Place
London W2 2BS
Tel: 020 7706 7682
By appointment only
Interior accessories,
tiebacks, trimmings
(Including Aqua and
Jewel Tieback p.42–43)

Peter Jones
Sloane Square
London SW1
Tel: 020 7730 3434
Phone for stores
(Including Denim Blind &
Curtain tiebacks p.84–85)

Remy Lemoine
Tel: 001 48 28 22 46
Phone for stockists
(Including Night and Day
Curtain tiebacks p.88–89)

SCREENS

Alison White
Ground Floor
Fitzpatrick Building
184–188 York Way
London N7 9AS
Tel: 020 7609 6127
By appointment only
Lights, blinds and rugs
(Including Standing
Screens p.7, p.98–99)

Silent Gliss
Tel: 01843 863571
www.silent-gliss.co.uk
Phone for further
information and
catalogues. Window
treatments, design
products, blinds (Including
Mesh Screen p.104–105)

GENERAL DETAIL

Artline
Tel: 020 7351 9908
Phone for stockists
(Including Country
Flannel Curtain poles,
brackets and hooks p.28–29)

See reference for Peter
Jones.(Including
equipment and heading
tape p.108–109)

Wemys Houless
1/20 Chelsea Harbour
Design Centre
London SW10 0XE
Tel: 020 7255 3305
sale@wemyshouless.co.uk
Public welcome. Decorative
accessories, trimmings
(Including Studded
Leather Blind studs
p.74–75)

BRACKETS, POLES, FINIALS AND CLIPS

Artisan
Tel: 020 7498 6974
Phone for stockists,
available at Peter Jones

Cracknell
Tel: 023 9223 1144
Phone for stockists,
available at Peter Jones

Resina Design
Tel: 01934 863535
Phone for stockists,
available at Peter Jones

PS Interiors
Tel: 0161 926 9398
Phone for stockists,
contract retailers
Major furniture
distributors

Bradley Collection
Tel: 01449722 724
Phone for brochure,
available at Peter Jones

GFC Lighting
Westminster Business Sq
London SE11 5JH
Tel: 020 7735 0677
mail@gfclighting.co.uk
Phone for further
information. Lighting
specialist, curtain
accessories

Spina
Tel: 020 7328 5274
Phone for stockists

STYLING ACCESSORIES

Malia
C2 & C3 The Chambers,
Chelsea Harbour, London
SW10 0XF
Tel: 020 7352 6656
Marble spheres
pp.66–67

**M.C.Stone & Flooring
Ltd**
69a Goldney Road,
London W9
Tel: 020 7289 7102
Wood flooring
pp.7, 98

London Lighting Co.,
135 Fulham Road,
London SW3
Tel: 020 7589 3612
Lamps
p.47

Ane Christensen
c/o Vessel, 114
Kensington Park Road,
London W11
Tel: 020 7727 8001
Artist
pp.66–67

Carden Cunietti
83 Westbourne Park Road,
London W2 5QH
Tel: 020 7229 8630
Polished silver vases
p.82

Bill Amberg
10 Chepstow Road,
London W2 5PD
Tel: 020 7727 3560
Leather flooring
p.29

INDEX

A

alpaca throw, 50–1, 140–1
aqua and jewel tieback, 42–3, 137–8
arched windows, 18, 48, 57
Austrian blinds, 62
awkward windows, 18–19

B

banners, 44–7, 139–40
bay windows, 18
 dress curtains, 48
 Roman blinds, 76–7, 148
binding strips, joining, 129
blackout lining, 34, 43, 72
blinds, 60–77
 Austrian blinds, 62
 awkward windows, 18
 combining styles, 78–89
 estimating fabric quantities, 122–3
 festoon blinds, 62
 flat blinds, 64–7, 144
 glass doors, 17
 headings, 37
 linings, 125–6
 measuring up, 121
 picture windows, 15
 roll-down blinds, 70–1, 145–6
 standard windows, 10
 studded leather blind, 74–5
 suiting and satin, 34–5, 134–5
 supports, 121–2
 tall windows, 13
 Venetian blinds, 62, 100
 see also roller blinds; Roman blinds
block fringes, 33
borders, curtains, 33
bow windows, 18
box headings, 37
box pelmets, 120, 127
brackets, poles, 110–11
brackets, tieback, 40, 116–17
buckram, box pelmets, 127
bullion fringes, 33

C

casement windows, 18
children's rooms, 84–5
circular windows, 18
clips, 37, 114–15
colour, fabrics, 26
cord: Italian stringing, 57
 tiebacks, 40
 trims, 33
corners, mitred, 128
country flannel curtain, 28–9, 131–2

curtain tape, 37
curtains, 22–59
 awkward windows, 18
 banners, 44–7, 139–40
 clips, hooks and rings, 114–15
 combining styles, 78–89
 country flannel curtain, 28–9, 131–2
 dress curtains, 48–51
 edgings and trims, 33–5, 131–2
 estimating fabric quantities, 122
 fabrics, 27–31
 glass doors, 17
 heading tapes, 37, 109
 headings, 24, 37–9
 layering, 86–9
 length, 24
 lined, 124–5
 measuring up, 120
 picture windows, 14–15
 poles and brackets, 110–11
 as room dividers, 100
 sheers, 52–9, 82–3
 standard windows, 10
 suiting and satin, 34–5, 134–5
 tall windows, 13
 tiebacks, 40–3, 116–17
 unlined, 123–4
 wall of silk, 30–1, 132–3
cutting out fabrics, 123

D

daisy chain stitch, 130
denim blind and curtain, 84–5, 150–2
doors: glass, 16–17
 sheer door panel, 102–3, 156–7
dormer windows, 18
dress curtains, 48–51

E

edgings, curtains, 33–5, 131–2
equipment, 108
eyelets: flat blinds, 64, 67
 headings, 37, 38–9, 136–7

F

fabrics: curtains, 27–31
 cutting out, 123
 estimating quantities, 122–3
 joining widths, 123
festoon blinds, 62
finials, 111, 112–13
flannel curtain, 28–9, 131–2
flat blinds, 64–7, 144
flat fell seams, 128
French pleat headings, 37, 42

French seams, 127
French windows, 17
 layering curtains, 89
 sheer door panel, 103
fringes, 33

G

gauze, sheers, 53
Georgian style, 13, 23, 53, 62
glass, and window size, 14
glass beads, silver beaded sheers, 58–9
glass doors, 16–17
goblet headings, 37
green fabric shutter, 96–7, 153

H

headings: blinds, 37
 curtains, 24, 37–9
 eyelet headings, 37, 38–9, 136–7
 heading tapes, 37, 109
herringbone stitch, 130
hooked panel blinds, 66–7, 144
hooks, 114–15

I

interlining, estimating fabric quantities, 122
Italian stringing, 57

J

Japan, 100

L

lace, 53–4, 86
ladder stitch, 129
lambrequins, 17
lapped seams, 128
layering curtains, 86–9
leather: studded leather blind, 74–5, 146–7
 trimmings, 28
lining: black-out lining, 34, 43, 72
 estimating fabric quantities, 122
 lined curtains, 124–5
 Roman blinds, 125–6
locking stitch, 130
louvred shutters, 91, 95

M

measuring up, 120–1
mesh screen, 104–5, 157
mitred corners, 128
muslin, sheers, 53, 54

N

net curtains, 53
night and day curtains, 88–9, 152

O

ombras, 116

P

panel blinds, 64–7, 144
pelmets, 23
 box pelmets, 127
 estimating fabric quantities, 122
 measuring, 120
 pelmet boards, 121
pencil-pleat headings, 37
picture windows, 14
poles, 110–11
 eyelet headings, 38–9, 136–7
 finials, 111, 112–13
 positioning, 120

R

radiators, 10, 13, 24
Regency style, 53
rings, 114–15
roll-down blinds, 70–1
roller blinds, 62, 68–71, 145–6
 positioning, 121
 as room dividers, 100
rolling blinds, 68–71, 145–6
Roman blinds, 43, 61, 62, 72–7
 bay windows, 76–7, 148
 combined with sheers, 82–3, 148–50
 denim blind, 84–5, 150–2
 estimating fabric quantities, 122–3
 lining, 125–6
 positioning, 121
 studded leather blind, 74–5, 146–7
 suiting and satin, 34–5, 134–5
 supports, 121–2
 with screens, 98–9
room dividers, 100–3
 mesh screen, 104–5, 157
rope tiebacks, 40

S

sash windows, 10, 23, 92
satin edgings, 34, 134–5
screens, 7, 91, 92, 94–5
 freestanding screens, 98–9, 100, 154–5
 mesh screen, 104–5, 157
 as room dividers, 100–1
seams, stitching, 127–8
sewing machines, 108
Shaker style, 65
sheers, 52–9
 combined with Roman blinds, 82–3, 148–50
 estimating fabric quantities, 122

layering, 86
long white sheer, 56–7, 142
 sheer door panel, 102–3, 156–7
 silver beaded sheers, 58–9, 143
shutters, 13, 91–3, 95
 green fabric shutter, 96–7, 153
silk, wall of, 30–1, 132–3
silver beaded sheers, 58–9, 143
skylights, 68
slipstitch, 130
standing screen, 98–9, 154–5
stitches, 129–30
stitching seams, 127–8
studded leather blind, 74–5, 146–7
suede trimmings, 28
suiting and satin curtains, 34–5, 134–5

T

tabs, 131
tall windows, 12–13, 48
tape: heading tapes, 37, 109
 touch-and-close tape, 57, 76, 109
tassels, 33, 116–17
tension wires, 111, 115
texture: fabrics, 26
 layering curtains, 86
throw, alpaca, 50–1, 140–1
tiebacks, 40–3, 116–17, 132
 aqua and jewel tieback, 42–3, 137–8
 measuring for, 121
tools, 108
touch-and-close tape, 57, 76, 109
tracks, positioning, 120
trims, curtains, 33–5
triple-pleat headings, 82

V

Venetian blinds, 62, 100
Victorian style, 23–4, 53, 91
voile, 54

W

weights, 129
wide windows, 14–15
windows: arched windows, 48, 57
 awkward windows, 18–19
 bay windows, 48, 76–7, 148
 glass doors, 16–17
 standard windows, 10–11
 tall windows, 12–13, 48
 wide windows, 14–15